louise rouledge

Science

KEY STAGE 2 PRACTICE

Alan Jarvis, Jean O'Sullivan, William Merrick

Published by Letts Educational
The Chiswick Centre
414 Chiswick High Road
London W4 5TF
020 89963333
020 87428390
mail@lettsed.co.uk
www.letts-education.com

Letts Educational Limited is a division of Granada Learning Limited, part of the Granada Media Group.

Text © Alan Jarvis, William Merrick, Joan O'Sullivan 2002

First published 2002

ISBN 1 84085 7102

The authors assert the moral right to be identified as the authors of this work.

British Library Cataloguing in Publication Data
A catalogue record for this book is available from the British Library.

Acknowledgements
The publishers would like to thank the following for permission to use copyright material. Every effort has been made to trace copyright holders and to obtain their permission for the use of copyright material. The author and publishers will gladly receive information enabling them to rectify any error or omission in subsequent editions.
Art Directors & Trip/Photo Library International 88 bl, Art Directors & Trip/Helene Rogers 42 tr, 44; Hulton Archive 88 tr; Bob Battersby 42 bl br, 52

Commissioned by Andrew Thraves
Project management by Kate Newport
Designed, edited and produced by Gecko Ltd, Cambridge
Cover design by Santamaria
Illustrations by Lizzie Harper, Margaret Jones, John Plumb, Peter and Janet Simmonett, Geoff Ward
Printed and bound by Ashford Colour Press

CONTENTS

How do I use the pages to revise?

Each topic is shown across two pages and is set out in the same way. It will help you to revise important facts, ideas and skills.

You have almost certainly come across all these ideas already in science. Use the pages to remind yourself about them and to check your understanding.

To revise a topic:

◆ Read the page slowly and carefully. Give yourself time to think about the ideas.

◆ Make sure you understand what everything means. If there is something you don't understand, ask someone who can help you with it.

◆ If possible, do the activity. It will help you to check your understanding.

◆ Read through the page again a few days later. This will help you to remember.

The left-hand box tells you more about the topic. Usually, it gives you an example of the science in everyday life so you can see how it works.

The left-hand introduction explains what the topic is about and introduces the important facts and ideas that you will need to remember.

FALLING THROUGH AIR

Why do some objects fall more slowly through the air than others? Two forces act on every falling object. Air resistance pushes up on the object but gravity pulls it down. If there were no air resistance, the object would fall quite quickly. When there is air resistance, it takes longer to fall. The size of the air resistance and the time it takes to fall are related.

● Friction is a pushing force. It pushes against moving objects.

● Air resistance is a friction force that slows down objects as they move through air.

● The bigger the air resistance, the slower an object falls.

Spot the two forces on these objects as they fall.

The force of gravity on the two pieces of paper is the same.

The flat sheet of paper has a larger surface area than a screwed-up one. It has greater air resistance which slows the sheet of paper down as it falls.

The screwed-up piece of paper has less air resistance which slows the fall down, but not nearly as much as with the sheet of paper.

A real parachute falls slowly through air. This is because the canopy has an extremely large surface area which has a very large air resistance. This greatly slows the rate at which it falls.

REMEMBER
Air resistance is the force slowing the parachute down. Don't use the word upthrust, it's not the same thing.

Draw a picture to explain what would happen to a coin and a feather when they fall on the Moon where there is no air resistance.

76

The REMEMBER box reminds you about a key point. Often it is something that many people get wrong or muddled.

The bullets give you the main ideas 'in a nutshell'. The red bullet is the simplest idea and the purple is the hardest.

The right-hand introduction focuses on one of the key skills in science. As well as knowing certain facts and ideas, you also need to have scientific skills such as:

- predicting;
- planning fair tests;
- interpreting graphs and tables;
- writing relationships;
- thinking about scientific evidence.

Writing a good relationship

When you do a fair test as part of an investigation, you usually end up with a conclusion which might be written something like this:

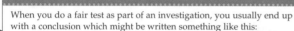

The bigger the air resistance, the longer it takes an object to fall.

This is called a relationship. To write a good relationship you need to say how one variable affects the other, using words like bigger and smaller.

Follow how Matthew learnt to write a good relationship.

Matthew did an investigation to find out the effect of weight on the time it took a spinner to fall. He made sure the test was fair. He kept the kind of spinner, and the height he dropped it from, the same. He only changed the number of paperclips on the spinner to increase its weight. Finally, he measured the time it took each spinner to fall and wrote the results in a table.

Number of paper clips on the spinner	1	2	3	4	5
Time taken to fall (s)	3	2.8	2.7	2.6	2.5

Then he wrote his first attempt at the relationship.

The spinner falls the quickest when five paperclips are put on it.

This is a true statement – but it doesn't explain the relationship. It only talks about one of the results, the last one in the table. Matthew looked again at the pattern in his results, and asked, 'When I change the number of paperclips, how does the time it takes the spinner to fall change?'

Then he tried to write the relationship again.

The lower the number of paperclips on the spinner, the longer it took to fall.

This is really good because it describes the pattern and tells you exactly how changing one factor (variable) affects the other. Can you see where he used 'er' words to help?

KEY WORDS

air resistance
gravity
factors
relationship

The right-hand box shows you the skill in action. Follow the description and see how the skill is useful when you do a scientific investigation.

The key words are ones that you need to know and use correctly when you write about this topic in science. Make sure you can spell each one and know what it means.

 Write a relationship that sums up how long parachutes of different sizes take to fall through air.

: **77**

The activities will help you to find out if you have understood the ideas and have mastered the skill. You may need to do some of them in the classroom, but many can be done at home.

TEETH AND THEIR CARE

Teeth are not all the same. They have different shapes for different jobs.
A diet that has a lot of sugar can increase the number of decayed teeth. You can show this with a bar chart.

- The shape of the teeth makes them useful for different purposes.
- If you do not take care of your teeth they will rot and have to be removed.
- The shape of an animal's teeth depends on its diet.

Humans have three different kinds of teeth.

Incisors are sharp for biting food.

Canines are pointed for holding and tearing.

Molars have flat tops for grinding.

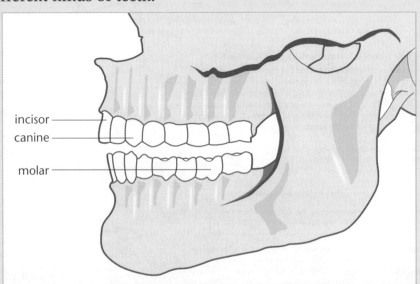

incisor
canine
molar

The main reason for tooth decay is the type of food a person eats. If you eat food with a lot of sugar, then the sugar stays on your teeth. Bacteria break down the sugars to form an acid that rots the teeth.

sugar + bacteria ➡ acid which causes decay

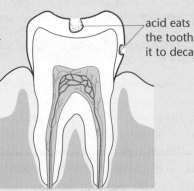

acid eats into the tooth causing it to decay

You can avoid tooth decay if you:

◆ make sure your diet is low in sugars – not too many sticky sweets and fizzy drinks;

◆ brush correctly after meals, particularly before you go to bed at night.

Look at labels on different types of food in tins and packets. Make a list of those containing sugar. Which foods contain little or no sugar?

Interpreting bar charts

You can find out information from a bar chart by looking for patterns and making comparisons. First you should look at the vertical axis to find out what sort of measurement is being used. Then look at the length of each bar. The longer the bar, the bigger the measurement.

Look at the bar chart of tooth decay.

In this bar chart, you can compare tooth decay for children with different amounts of sugar in their diet. The amount of tooth decay is measured by the number of filled teeth.

Low
A low-sugar diet with very few sweets or fizzy drinks

Medium
A medium-sugar diet with some sweets and some fizzy drinks

High
A high-sugar diet with sweets and fizzy drinks taken every day

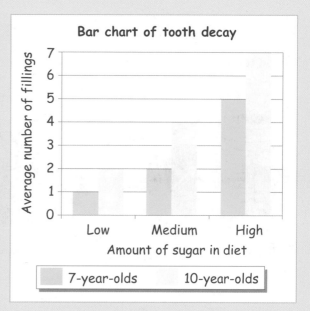

Bar chart of tooth decay

Look at the dark yellow bars. These show the average numbers of decayed teeth for 7-year-olds. You can see that the number of decayed teeth increases as the amount of sugar in their diets increases.

Now look at the light yellow bars. Can you see that they show the same pattern for the 10-year-olds? The more sugar they eat, the greater the number of decayed teeth.

Now look at the two bars for low sugar. This shows that, on average, 10-year-olds have more decayed teeth than 7-year-olds. You will find the same pattern for medium- and high-sugar diets.

KEY WORDS

incisor
canine
molar
decay

Explain why 10-year-olds generally have greater numbers of decayed teeth than 7-year-olds.

DIETS

Your diet must include food for activity, food for growth and repair, and foods to keep you healthy. A balanced diet provides the correct proportions of these different types of food.

- All animals need food. Different animals have different diets.
- Starches, sugars and fats provide energy for activity. Fish, meat, dairy products and some types of vegetables provide protein which is needed for growth and repair. Fruit and vegetables keep you healthy.

Do you think you have a healthy diet? This is what you need.

Food for energy for activity	Food for growth and repair	Food to keep you healthy

Starches, sugars and fats   Protein   Fruit and vegetables

A balanced diet has suitable amounts of each type of food like the ones shown here.

Vegetarians can get protein from other sources such as nuts, beans and lentils instead of meat and fish.

Overweight people need to eat less and avoid foods with high fat and sugar. It also helps to do more exercise.

Children and teenagers need more protein foods for growth.

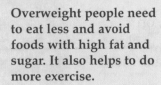

8

 Design a menu for a meal that would fit in with a balanced diet.

Using data on a graph to predict the next results

When you study a graph you may be asked to predict what readings would come next. Remember that a graph shows a pattern. Once you have worked out the pattern, you can predict what reading is likely to come next.

Look at this graph and see if you can predict the next readings.

The doctor told Matthew's dad that he must lose some weight because being overweight was making him unhealthy.

He decided that he would eat less fatty food, have more fruit and vegetables and take more exercise.

He weighed himself every week. This graph shows how his weight has changed.

What pattern does this line graph show?

You can see that the line is going down which shows that overall his weight is decreasing.

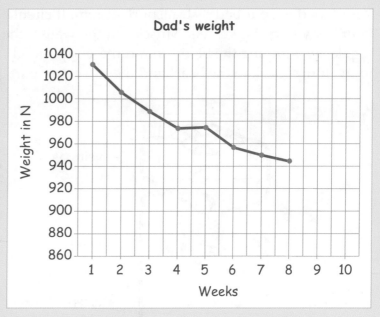

Graph showing changing weight

If Matthew's dad continued with his healthier diet and exercise, can you use the graph to predict what he would weigh by week 10?

Of course, you cannot give an exact figure. But you can see that the line of the graph is going down, so it is likely that his weight would have decreased again. It would probably be between 930 and 940 N.

KEY WORDS

balanced diet
predicting

Why do you think Matthew's dad weighed more in week 5?

HEART AND CIRCULATION

The heart acts as a pump to move blood around the body. It beats about 70 times every minute throughout your life. During exercise the heart works harder to pump more blood to the muscles. You can measure your pulse to find out the rate of your heartbeat.

- The pulse rate is a measure of how fast the heart is beating.
- During exercise the heart beats faster to take blood quickly to the muscles.
- In an investigation into pulse rate, repeated measurements should be made and several people should be used to obtain reliable results.

Study this diagram of the heart and blood vessels.

Your blood is your body's transport system. It circulates to all parts of your body in blood vessels. Muscles in the wall of the heart contract regularly, pumping the blood round the body. Blood goes from the heart to the lungs, back to the heart and then to every part of your body.

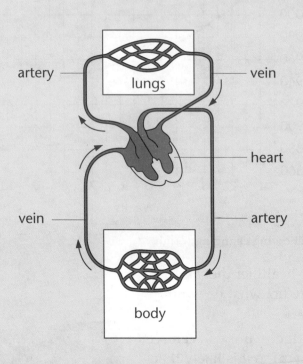

The blood transports many different substances. For example oxygen is collected in the lungs and taken to all parts of your body. Digested food has to be taken from your intestines to other parts of your body.

Muscles need a large blood supply as they have to work hard, particularly when you exercise. That is why your heart beats faster when you exercise.

In your wrist, you should be able to feel an artery which 'ticks' each time your heart beats. This is your pulse.

Follow the arrows in the diagram and you will see that blood flows to the heart in veins and away from the heart in arteries.

 Find your pulse and measure its rate (number of beats in a minute). Then jump up and down for 1 minute and measure it again. What do your results show?

Using line graphs to identify patterns in results

When we draw line graphs we usually put the units of measurement on the vertical axis (the y-axis) and the information about the readings along horizontal axis (the x-axis). Quite often, the x-axis shows time.

Look at the graph of pulse rate and identify any patterns it shows.

The pulse is measured at different times, so the time is placed on the x-axis and the pulse rate on the y-axis.

This is what happened when Clare's pulse was measured every 4 hours for one day.

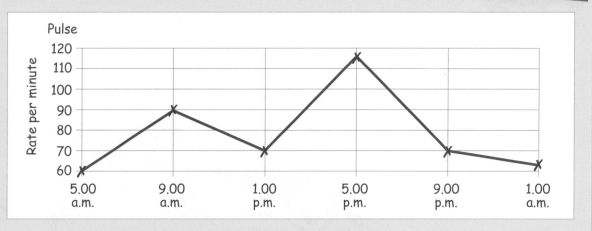

Graph of changing pulse rate

These are some of the activities Clare carried out during the day:

◆ sleeping;

◆ running;

◆ walking;

◆ sitting down.

For a graph like this, you could be asked to match these activities with times of day from the graph and then to give reasons for your answers.

Running is the most energetic activity

and for this the heart would need to beat very fast to supply more blood to the muscles. On the graph, the highest pulse rate was at 5.00 p.m. so this is likely to be the time when Clare was running.

Walking is less energetic than running but more energetic than sitting or sleeping so it is likely that the second fastest pulse rate at 9.00 a.m was when Clare was walking.

In the same way you could say that Clare was probably sitting down at 1.00 p.m. and 9.00 p.m. and sleeping at 1.00 a.m. and 5.00 a.m..

Look at the graph and then write a diary for Clare's day from morning to night time.

THE SKELETON

Your skeleton is made up of bones. These are hard and strong to support the softer parts of the body. The skull protects the brain and the rib cage protects the heart and lungs.

- Humans have bony skeletons inside their bodies.
- The skeleton supports and protects the body.
- Your skeleton grows as you grow.

Study this skeleton to find out the names and functions of some of the bones.

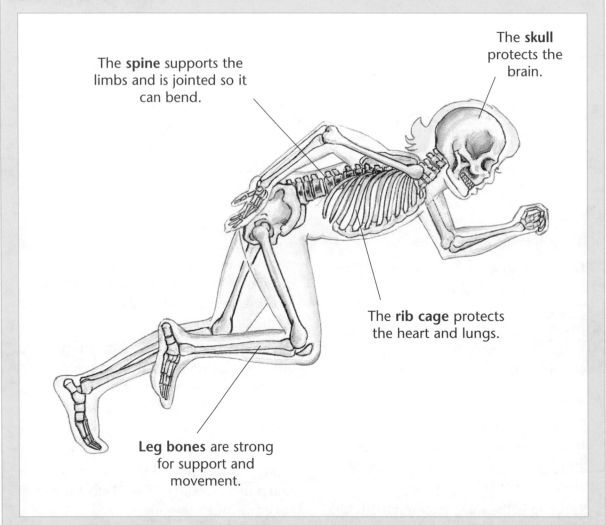

The **spine** supports the limbs and is jointed so it can bend.

The **skull** protects the brain.

The **rib cage** protects the heart and lungs.

Leg bones are strong for support and movement.

 Draw round your hand. Now feel your hand and bend your fingers to find out where the bones are. Draw the bones inside the outline.

Interpreting a graph

Line graphs are useful for finding patterns. They can tell you when something is happening quickly or slowly. A steep slope tells you that the change is faster or greater. When the line flattens then there is no further change.

Look at this line graph of Daniel's growth.

This line graph shows Daniel's growth. Every two years Daniel's height was measured. The graph shows the pattern of growth from 0 to 24 years.

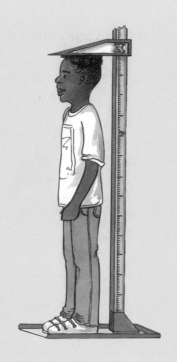

Graph showing Daniel's height

On a graph like this, you could be asked questions like these.

◆ **When did Daniel grow most quickly?**
To answer this correctly, look at the graph and find the steepest slope. You can see that this is between 0 and 2 years.

◆ **When did Daniel stop growing in height?**
Find out when the line flattens. Go back to the point where there is no further increase in height and read the age from the x-axis. You can use a ruler to help. You will find that the line flattens at 20 years.

◆ **Why did the readings for height start at 50, not at 0?**
This type of graph would not start at 0 because Daniel measured 50 cm when he was born.

 Measure your height in cm. Then measure the other people in your family. Put your results into a bar chart.

- You have muscles attached to bones.
- To move you need both a skeleton and muscles.
- Muscles work in pairs; when one contracts another relaxes.

When you move, a muscle between two bones contracts or gets shorter. This pulls the bones together. To move the bones apart, a different muscle contracts and the first muscle relaxes.

Try bending your arm to see what happens to your muscles.

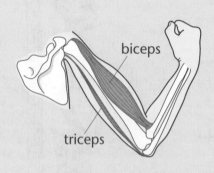

When you bend your arm your biceps contracts. The muscle gets shorter and pulls the bones together. At the same time your triceps relaxes.

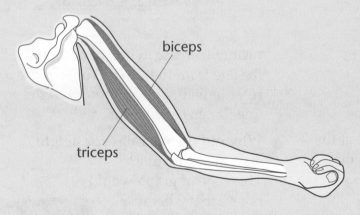

When you straighten your arm the opposite happens. The triceps contracts and at the same time the biceps muscle relaxes.

Muscles always work in pairs – when one contracts, the other relaxes. Different pairs move each part of your body.

REMEMBER
When a muscle contracts, it gets shorter. When it relaxes, it goes back to its original length.

 Can you work out where the muscles will be: • to bend and straighten your finger • to nod your head • to open and close your mouth?

Making good observations

It is not always possible to make accurate measurements.
For some investigations, you may be able to get the information
you need from good observations.

How do you feel when you have been running fast?

I feel tired.

I breathe a lot faster.

I feel hot when I run fast.

I think my muscles work harder - that is why I feel tired.

The group decided to run round the playground for 5 minutes and then decide if they were hot, breathing faster or feeling tired. After 10 minutes sitting down they asked themselves the same questions.

	After 5 minutes exercise			After 10 minutes sitting still		
	Hot	Tired	Panting	Hot	Tired	Panting
Sara	✔	✗	✔	✗	✗	✗
Mina	✔	✔	✔	✗	✗	✗
Matthew	✔	✔	✔	✗	✗	✗
Yasmin	✔	✔	✔	✔	✗	✗
Daniel	✔	✗	✔	✗	✗	✗

The group concluded that:

> When we exercise we become hot, tired and breathe more quickly because our muscles have to work harder.

But remember, you can only draw conclusions from reliable results. How reliable are their results? They did not all report the same feelings.

Sara and Daniel said they were not tired after running for 5 minutes. Perhaps they are fitter. Yasmin said she was still hot after resting for 10 minutes. It can be difficult for people to decide how they feel without taking measurements.

Scientists get round this problem by using much larger numbers of people or by taking more measurements.

KEY WORDS

muscles
contract
relax

What measurements would make the evidence more reliable in this investigation?

KEEPING HEALTHY

- Some drugs are harmful.
- Substances like alcohol, tobacco and other drugs can affect the way the body functions and these effects can be harmful.
- Medicines can be harmful if they are not taken according to instructions.

Most people like to be healthy and so avoid doing things that would be bad for their health. Some people do things that are very harmful or even dangerous – things such as smoking cigarettes, drinking too much alcohol, overeating and taking drugs that are not needed.

Look at these pictures. They all show possible dangers to your health.

Smokers are more likely to suffer from heart disease, lung cancer, bronchitis and other diseases of the lungs.

Drinking too much alcohol harms the liver and the brain. A person driving after drinking too much alcohol can cause accidents.

Medicines given by a doctor are necessary when you are ill. Taking medicines that are not needed can cause serious harm.

Eating too much fatty food and not taking enough exercise can cause serious heart problems.

Make two lists with these headings: • Things we must do to stay healthy • Things we must avoid to stay healthy

Using charts and graphs to make comparisons

By putting information into a chart or graph you can compare different sets of results for different groups.

Look at the chart and the graph.

Bar chart showing the effect of alcohol on reaction time

What pattern can you see in this bar chart?

It shows the effect of drinking alcohol on reaction time. You can see that the more alcohol someone drinks, the slower their reaction time.

This means that a car driver who has had alcohol can take longer to brake. This could well lead to an accident.

Line graph showing the effect of smoking on the risk of dying from lung cancer

Can you see the pattern in this graph?

It shows the effect of smoking on the risk of dying. For example, people who smoke 20 cigarettes a day are 15 times more likely to die of lung cancer than non-smokers. You can see from this graph that the more cigarettes people smoke each day, the greater their risk of dying from an illness caused by smoking.

It was only when these figures were gathered and graphs like this one were drawn, that people first realised smoking was the main cause of lung cancer.

KEY WORDS

alcohol
tobacco
drugs

 Redraw the graph and extend the axes. Can you predict the increased risk for a group of people who smoke 50 cigarettes each day?

PLANT GROWTH

All living things grow. In order to grow they need food. Only green plants make their own food. Animals cannot do this.

- Plants need light, warmth and water to grow.
- To measure how a plant grows you can measure its height.
- To get reliable results you need to measure a number of plants, not just one.

Look at these plants. They have been grown under different conditions.

This plant is growing well. It has warmth, water and light.

This plant has warmth and light but no water. Without water it cannot grow. The leaves and stem wilt and then die.

This plant has water and warmth but has been kept in the dark. Without light the plant cannot make food. All growth stops, the leaves turn yellow and after a few days the plant will die.

Why do you think some plants do not grow well even when they have light, water and warmth?

Obtaining reliable evidence

You need reliable evidence before you can draw any conclusions from an investigation. If an investigation has not been well planned, it may not produce enough evidence to draw any conclusions.

Look at this investigation. Do you think the evidence collected will be reliable?

The class have been asked to find out how much water a plant needs to grow well.

I will water my plant three times a day.

Sara, Matthew, Tom and Mina have decided to use sunflower seeds and to keep their plants in the school greenhouse.

I am also going to water mine once a day.

I will water my plant once a week.

I will water mine once a day.

These are their results after five weeks.

Name	Watered	Growth in height
Sara	once a week	54 cm
Matthew	three times a day	26 cm
Tom	once a day	0 cm
Mina	once a day	96 cm

Do you think their evidence is reliable?

Look at the results for Tom's and Mina's sunflowers. You can see that they have very different results even though they treated their plants in the same way. Whose result is correct?

Of course we cannot be sure, but perhaps Tom's seed had a disease and could not grow. Not every seed will grow into a new plant.

It is clear that they needed to use more plants for their investigation to provide more reliable evidence.

KEY WORDS

growth
food
evidence

Plan this investigation again, giving details of how you would obtain reliable evidence.

PARTS OF A PLANT

All flowering plants have roots, stems and leaves. The roots are usually in the soil and the stem holds the leaves above the ground. The leaves use light from the sun to help make food for the plant.

- Plants need healthy roots, stems and leaves to grow well.
- Without healthy roots, a stem and leaves, a plant could not take up water or make food.
- Green plants use light to make material for new growth from air and water.

Look carefully at this diagram of a plant.

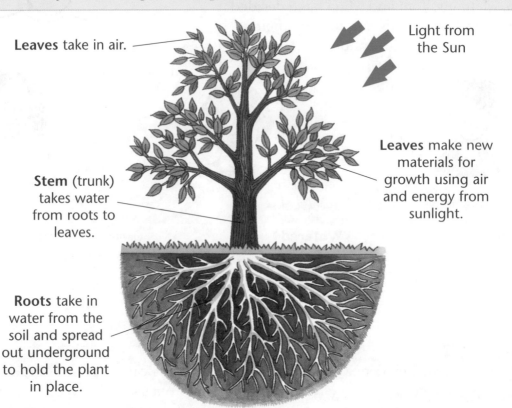

Leaves take in air.

Light from the Sun

Leaves make new materials for growth using air and energy from sunlight.

Stem (trunk) takes water from roots to leaves.

Roots take in water from the soil and spread out underground to hold the plant in place.

REMEMBER
Only plants can make their own food.

Remember this word equation. It shows the main function of leaves.

$$air + water \xrightarrow{\text{light}} \text{new materials for growth}$$

 Carefully dig up a weed. First make sure it is a weed! Find its roots, stem and leaves. How is each part designed to do its job well?

Making accurate observations

When you carry out an investigation it is important to make accurate observations. You need to look carefully and then make clear diagrams and written comments.

Look at how Mina made observations about what happens when water moves up a stem.

Mina selected a young piece of celery stalk with a leaf and placed it in a solution of ink and water. She made sure that only the bottom end of the stalk was in the liquid. She made careful drawings of the experiment.

After two hours she could see that parts of the leaf had turned red.

She examined it carefully and made a drawing to show which parts were red. She also cut through the stalk to find out which parts had turned red and made another drawing of the stalk.

These are her drawings and notes on what she had observed.

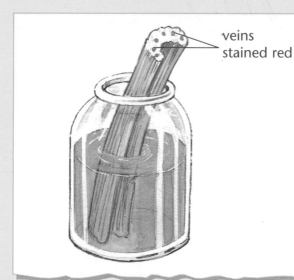

veins stained red

After 1 hour I removed the leaves and looked at the cut stalk. Only the veins inside had turned red.

The veins of the leaf are also red.

What conclusions do you think Mina could draw from her observations?

She studied her drawings and then decided that the water inside the celery only travels through special tubes. She also concluded that these tubes run from the stalk into the leaf, where they can be seen as leaf veins.

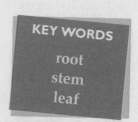

KEY WORDS

root
stem
leaf

Make a careful drawing of a plant to show its roots, stem and leaves. Put arrows on your drawing to show which way the water travels in the plant.

LIFE CYCLES

Each kind of living thing needs to reproduce (make new individuals) if the species is to carry on. Many plants do this by flowering. The plant produces flowers that produce seeds that will then grow into new plants. The life cycle of a flowering plant can be shown in a flow chart.

- Each part of a flower has a different function.
- Flowers must be pollinated and fertilised before they can make seeds.

REMEMBER
You need to learn the names of the parts of the flower and know what they do.

Look at this drawing showing the inside of a flower.

Petals are brightly coloured to attract insects.

Stamens make the **pollen**.

Sepals hold the flower together.

The **stigma** is sticky so that pollen grains stick to it.

The **style** connects the stigma to the ovary.

The **ovary** is where the seed will develop after fertilisation.

What is pollination?

This is when pollen lands on the stigma.

Pollen is often carried from the stamens to the stigma by wind or insects.

Flowers pollinated by insects have brightly coloured petals and scent to attract the insects.

REMEMBER
The plural of ovum is ova!

They also produce nectar which is a sugary substance that bees and other insects feed on.

Flowers pollinated by wind have no brightly coloured petals and no scent or nectar.

What is fertilisation?

The pollen from the stigma has to fertilise the ovum inside the ovary. Only then can a seed develop.

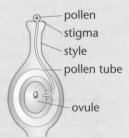

- pollen
- stigma
- style
- pollen tube
- ovule

 Find a group of flowers in a garden. Watch any insects like bees or butterflies that visit the flowers. Make notes on what happens and compare them with a friend.

Interpreting a flow chart

Flow charts help you to show a sequence of events. They can be used in many different situations. Not all flow charts are in cycles. Some have a beginning and an end, like a food chain.

You can display the life cycle of a flowering plant using a flow chart.

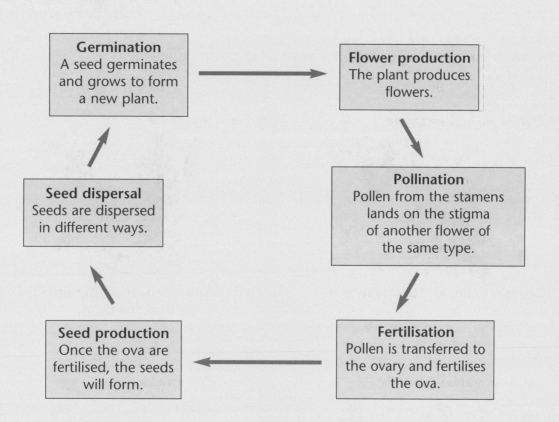

You can start at any point on the flow chart and then follow the arrows round to explain each of the stages. You may be given the names of the stages and asked to arrange them into a correct sequence or you may be asked to fill in missing words.

The life cycles of other living things can also be arranged as a flow chart. For instance, humans have a simple life cycle but some animals, like butterflies and frogs, have more complicated ones.

KEY WORDS

pollination
fertilisation
flow chart

Arrange these stages to show a human life cycle:
• adult • baby • teenager • toddler

SEED DISPERSAL AND GERMINATION

Seeds produced by plants are dispersed or scattered. Once they have been dispersed, they can germinate. This means they start to grow into new plants. If all the seeds fell close to the parent plant, the new plants would be overcrowded and most would die.

- Wind, animals or explosion can disperse seeds.
- In investigations with seeds, you should use a number of seeds to get reliable results.
- You can only draw good conclusions from reliable results.

Do you remember the different ways that seeds are dispersed?

By wind

Dandelion and sycamore

Seeds are light and blown away in the wind.

By explosion

Lupin and gorse

Pods burst open when ripe and fling seeds away from the plant.

By animals

Cleavers and burdock

Seed cases have hooks which stick to animals' fur.

Rose hip and elderberry

Birds eat the fruits. The seeds then go through the gut and are passed out in their droppings.

 Look round a garden or park and see if you can find any fruits producing seeds. Can you work out how the seeds are dispersed?

Using reliable evidence to draw conclusions

If you get only one set of measurements, or carry out only one reading, your results may not be accurate. You need reliable evidence before you can draw conclusions.

KEY WORDS

seed dispersal
germination
reliable results

Look at the evidence obtained in this investigation.

The class were asked to carry out an investigation to find out what conditions seeds need in order to germinate.

This table shows the number of seeds that germinated.

	Number of seeds	No water	In fridge	In dark	In light
Group 1	1 seed in each condition	0	1	0	1
Group 2	10 seeds in each condition	0	2	9	8
Group 3	100 seeds in each condition	0	8	93	89

How reliable are these results?

Not every seed in a packet will germinate. When only one seed is used it may be one of those that is not healthy, so the results of group 1 are not reliable. It is not possible to draw any conclusions from this set of results.

Groups 2 and 3 both have reliable results. 100 seeds would be better than 10, but would take much longer to count and set up. There was also not much difference between the two sets of results.

Using the reliable results from either group 2 or group 3, the class could conclude that seeds need water and warmth to germinate. They could also see that there was very little difference between the numbers germinating in the light and in the dark. They could therefore conclude that light does not affect germination.

Why do you think gardeners wanting to grow a row of peas will often put more than one pea seed into each hole?

KEYS

Keys are used to sort animals or plants into their correct group or to identify them. Some keys are very simple with just a few animals or plants – others may need a whole book.

You can work out the names of these shore birds using the branching key.

A   B   C   D

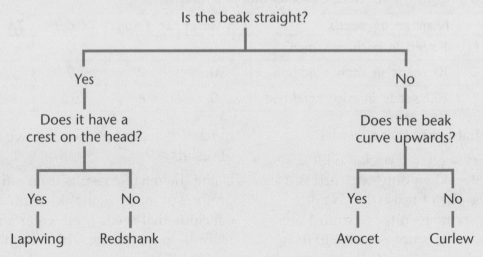

Is the beak straight?

Yes   No

Does it have a crest on the head?   Does the beak curve upwards?

Yes   No   Yes   No

Lapwing   Redshank   Avocet   Curlew

Look at bird A. Start at the top and answer each question. Follow the correct lines down until you come to the name of a bird. Bird A is the only one that does not have a straight beak that does not curve upwards. This makes it a curlew.

Now identify the other three birds, B, C and D. Which features did you use to identify each one?

Using a key correctly

Keys are easy to use. Look at the animal or plant you want to identify. Then answer each question in turn and follow the instructions until you come to its name.

Here is a key to identify some freshwater fish.

You will see that it has been set out differently. This sort is called a numbered key.

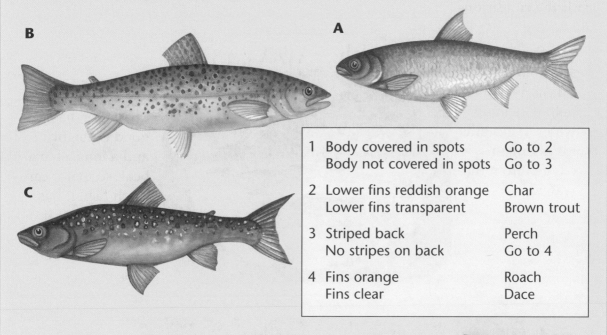

1	Body covered in spots	Go to 2
	Body not covered in spots	Go to 3
2	Lower fins reddish orange	Char
	Lower fins transparent	Brown trout
3	Striped back	Perch
	No stripes on back	Go to 4
4	Fins orange	Roach
	Fins clear	Dace

Jamal was asked to identify the fish using the key. This was how he worked out the name of fish A.

KEY WORDS

branching key
numbered key

He looked at fish A and the first statement. Does it have spots?

No – it does not have spots.

He then moved on to 3. Does it have a striped back?

No - it does not have a striped back.

He then moved to 4. Are the fins orange or clear?

The fins are clear so the fish is a dace.

You can see how Jamal has identified the first fish correctly.

 Use the key to identify the other two fish in the same way.

HABITATS

Habitats are places where animals and plants live. Each living thing is suited to the environment where it lives. This is called adaptation. Choice chambers can be used to collect evidence about the conditions animals prefer in their habitats.

- Different plants and animals live in different habitats such as ponds, woods and hedges.
- Animals and plants are adapted to their habitats.

Compare these two habitats. How are the animals adapted to suit the conditions?

The fish has a streamlined body, fins and a tail to help it swim in water. It has gills for taking in oxygen from the water.

The heron has good eyesight and a long, sharp beak so that it can catch fish. It has wings so that it can fly to other ponds and rivers to search for food.

The squirrel has claws to help it grip branches so that it can run and jump through the trees. It has sharp teeth for cracking nuts.

The deer is camouflaged so that it can hide in the undergrowth. It has long legs so that it can run away quickly from danger.

Name two other habitats. If you can, choose ones near where you live. Choose one animal from each and describe how it is suited to live there.

Choosing what evidence to collect

When you plan an investigation, it is important to decide on the sort of evidence you need to collect. You might make accurate observations, or you might take careful measurements.

Did Tom choose a good way to collect evidence?

How can I find out if woodlice prefer damp or dry places?

Look at how Tom did his investigation.

Do woodlice prefer damp or dry places?

I will put 10 woodlice in a box with a dry end and a damp end.

I will count how many woodlice are at each end every 2 minutes.

I will take readings for 20 minutes.

I will make sure my test is fair by keeping everything else the same.

My apparatus

woodlice — mesh
dry cotton wool — damp cotton wool

Table for my results

| Time (mins) | Numbers of woodlice | |
	Wet end	Dry end
0		
2		
4		

You can see that Tom will be able to collect evidence from this experiment to find out if woodlice prefer dry or damp places.

This is not the only way he could have done it. Instead he could:

◆ measure how long one woodlouse stayed at each end;

◆ watch how all the woodlice behaved in the choice chamber and make notes.

Choose a different method for obtaining evidence in this investigation and write up your plan to show what you would do.

LIVING TOGETHER

Each habitat has plants and animals that depend on each other. You may remember some habitats that you have studied such as ponds, woods and hedges. If a habitat changes it will affect the animals and plants that live there. For instance, if a pond is drained, all the animals that lived in it will die.

- Different plants and animals live in different habitats.
- Animals depend on plants for food and shelter.
- Plants depend on animals for nutrients and help in pollen and seed dispersal.

Think about how animals and plants are interdependent.

How does the tree help the bird?

- ◆ The tree provides food such as seeds and insects.

- ◆ The bird uses the tree to build its nest to protect its eggs and young from danger.

- ◆ The bird flies into the tree to escape from predators and sleeps there at night.

How does the bird help the tree?

- ◆ Birds may eat the berries and the birds' droppings will help scatter the seeds away from the tree.

- ◆ The droppings will help to put nutrients back into the soil that the tree will need for growth.

How do plants help the earthworm?

- ◆ The earthworm feeds on dead plant material such as fallen leaves.

How does the earthworm help the plants?

- ◆ The earthworms make tunnels in the soil which improves the drainage and allows air to enter. This helps the roots of plants get water and air from the soil more easily and so helps them to grow better.

- ◆ The earthworms help to break down dead animal and plant matter by eating it. The earthworms' droppings then put the nutrients back into the soil in a form that the plants can use for growth.

How do earthworms help animals?

- ◆ Earthworms are an important food source for animals such as birds, moles and hedgehogs.

 Write down ways in which fish in a pond help the pondweed to grow and how the pondweed helps the fish to live.

Predicting the effect of a change

You may be asked to predict what will happen next when something is changed. You should always try to give reasons for your predictions.

Think about some ways we could change a habitat.

We could:

◆ cut down a hedge;

◆ drain a pond;

◆ drain a marsh;

◆ dig up grassland;

◆ cut down woodland;

◆ flood farmland with seawater.

Mr Jones owns a small woodland which has a variety of different trees with bluebells and other shade-loving plants. Many insects, birds and small mammals such as shrews and squirrels live and feed in the wood. Mr Jones has decided he wants to cut down the trees to plant a field of potatoes.

This is what some of the class thought would happen.

I think all the birds would fly away.

All the bluebells would die because they would not have the shade they need.

All the insects would die because they would not have the right food.

Some of the animals would eat potatoes instead.

The predictions that include **because…** are better.
These all include a reason.

A really good prediction would be:

> The animals will die or move away because the conditions will no longer be suitable for woodland animals. All the shade-loving plants will die **because** there are no trees to shade them.

KEY WORDS

interdependent
prediction

Choose one of the other changes listed above and predict what would happen to the animals and plants in the habitat. Try to use 'because' in your prediction.

FEEDING RELATIONSHIPS

- Some animals feed on plants and others feed on animals.
- Food chains show feeding relationships in a habitat.
- Nearly all food chains start with a green plant.

All living things need food. Plants are able to make their own food but animals have to find theirs. You need to know about some of the animals that eat other animals and be able to name some of the animals that only eat plants. You can use this information to construct a food chain.

Here is one food chain.

grass ⟶ rabbit ⟶ fox

Food chains almost always start with a plant – in this one it is grass. The plant is called a producer, because it makes or produces the food. The rabbit eats the grass, so this comes next. The rabbit is a consumer because it eats or consumes the grass. The fox eats the rabbit so it is also a consumer.

An animal that hunts and feeds on other animals is called a predator and the animal that is caught and eaten is the prey. In this food chain, the fox is the predator and the rabbit is its prey.

The arrows in a food chain always point towards the animal which does the eating. An arrow means 'is eaten by'.

REMEMBER
Plants make their food using sunlight, but the Sun is not food. So almost all food chains start with a plant.

Here is a list of predators and a list of prey. Pair up each prey with a predator.
Predators: • robin • mole • fox • spider • heron • owl
Prey: • mouse • fish • fly • rabbit • earthworm • caterpillar

Constructing food chains

To construct a food chain you need to know the names of the animals and plants in it and what each of them eats. Then you can use this information to arrange them in the right order.

Look at the way Sara constructed a food chain.

These are some of the animals and plants she found in her garden.

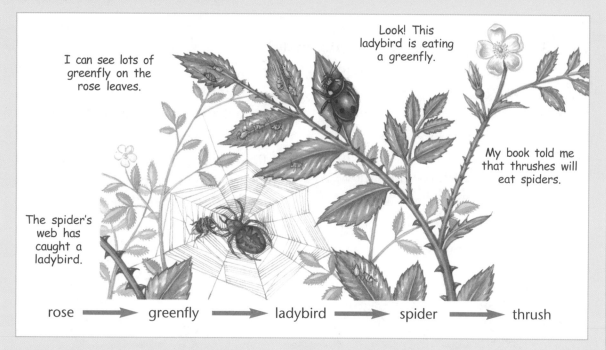

I can see lots of greenfly on the rose leaves.

Look! This ladybird is eating a greenfly.

My book told me that thrushes will eat spiders.

The spider's web has caught a ladybird.

rose ➡ greenfly ➡ ladybird ➡ spider ➡ thrush

This is Sara's food chain. You can see that the greenfly is eating the rose leaf, so the rose leaf must start the food chain. Sara then looked to see what was eating the greenfly. It was the ladybird, so this came next. She continued in this way until she completed her food chain.

Food chains usually start with a plant, but it doesn't have to be the leaves. Many animals eat other parts of a plant. All of these could be the first food in a food chain:

◆ nectar or pollen from the flower;

◆ sap from the stem;

◆ seeds and fruits;

◆ dead leaves.

KEY WORDS

producer
consumer
predator
prey

Make up two food chains of your own. Use animals and plants from this list:
• grass • cow • human • frog • greenfly • worm • lettuce • snail • spider
• fox • rabbit

HARMFUL MICRO-ORGANISMS

What causes illness? We know that some diseases are caused by micro-organisms or germs that live and grow inside our bodies. We can collect information to find out how germs are passed from one person to another.

- Very small living things called micro-organisms can cause illness.
- Micro-organisms feed, grow and reproduce like other organisms.
- Micro-organisms can move from one food source to another and cause food poisoning.

How do micro-organisms get into your body?

You cannot see micro-organisms with the naked eye because they are so small. Here are just a few of the ways that they can get into our bodies.

- Micro-organisms can be passed from one person to another when they talk, cough or sneeze.
- Germs on hands can be passed to food.
- Micro-organisms can be spread from raw meat onto other food if you are not careful to use different knives or chopping boards, for example.
- Micro-organisms can be spread by flies – if food is not covered, a fly may land on it, bringing germs.

Flies can carry germs onto the food you eat. The germs can make you ill.

If harmful micro-organisms get into our bodies, they can make us ill.

You may have had the disease chickenpox. This spreads very quickly from one person to another and very often several people in a class will get the illness at the same time. You can probably think of some other illnesses that spread in a similar way.

 Make a list of ways you can avoid diseases caused by micro-organisms.

Choosing how to collect evidence

Scientists often carry out experiments to collect evidence but this is not the only way. Asking people questions and interpreting their answers can be another way of collecting evidence.

Here is another way of obtaining evidence.

There had been an outbreak of food poisoning in the village school. The doctors wanted to know where the micro-organisms had come from so they decided to ask all the children the same questions. They knew that the germs had probably come from meat, fish or eggs.

The first question was, 'What food have you eaten in the last three days?'

Name	Chicken	Eggs	Beefburger	Fish
Daniel	✔	✔	✔	✗
Sara	✗	✔	✔	✗
Yasmin	✔	✗	✔	✔
Clare	✔	✔	✔	✗
Tom	✔	✗	✔	✔
Matthew	✔	✔	✔	✗

> **KEY WORDS**
> micro-organisms
> microbes
> germs

You can see from this information that the one food they had all eaten was the beefburger. The doctors thought this was the likely source of infection.

They then needed to find out where the infected beefburgers had come from.

So next they asked, 'Where did you eat the beefburgers?'

Name	At home	School dinners	Take-away	Party	Cafe
Daniel	✔	✗	✔	✔	✗
Sara	✗	✗	✔	✗	✔
Yasmin	✗	✗	✔	✗	✗
Clare	✗	✔	✔	✗	✔
Tom	✔	✔	✔	✔	✗
Matthew	✔	✔	✔	✗	✗

Because the only place that they had all eaten a beefburger was from a take-away, it seems likely that this was the source of the outbreak.

This is a different way of obtaining evidence. It can be very useful, particularly when you can ask the same questions to a large number of people.

 What other questions would they need to ask the children to find the source of the infected beefburgers?

USEFUL MICRO-ORGANISMS

We know that some micro-organisms are harmful but in fact most are useful. For instance micro-organisms are necessary for dead plants and animals to decay. Imagine what the world would be like if nothing decayed! Other micro-organisms are useful in the food we eat. Yeasts are micro-organisms which are needed to make bread and wine.

- Micro-organisms which cause decay are doing a useful job.
- Investigations with yeast show that it is a living organism.

Micro-organisms are useful in lots of ways.

If dead plants and animals did not decay, the nutrients inside them would not be released into the soil. Eventually there would be no nutrients for plant growth and all living things in the world would die.

You can see that the process of decay is essential for life to continue. If there were no decay, the world would be covered with dead plants and animals.

Because these micro-organisms are everywhere, they will also be on any food we keep. If this is kept for too long, it will also decay.

Yeast is a micro-organism which we need to make bread. When yeast is added to sugar it produces small bubbles of gas. This gas in the dough makes the bread rise.

Micro-organisms are also needed to make yoghurt and cheese.

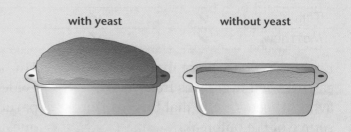

with yeast   without yeast

Find out about useful micro-organisms. List as many things as you can that could not happen if there were no micro-organisms.

Identifying factors needed for a fair test

In an investigation, you must decide what factor you are measuring and then keep everything else the same.

**Look at this investigation planned by Topi.
Do you think it is a fair test?**

Topi was asked to find out what conditions yeast needs to grow well.

This is what she did.

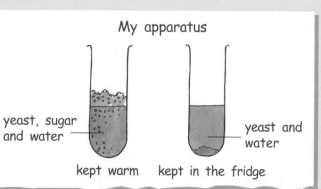

I want to find out the best conditions for growing yeast.

I will put yeast, sugar and water into one tube and keep it warm. In another tube I will put yeast and water and put it in the fridge.

I will see which one produces bubbles.

My apparatus

yeast, sugar and water

yeast and water

kept warm   kept in the fridge

This is not a fair test. Can you see why?

Topi did not keep all the factors the same – she kept a tube with yeast, sugar and water in a warm place but not a similar one in the fridge. She put a tube with just yeast and water in the warm place but she did not put one like it in the fridge.

We can say that she did not keep all the factors or variables the same.

Would it make it fairer if Topi did this same experiment more than once?

No, it would not help! As this investigation is not a fair test it would not make it fairer to do the same things more than once. You must change the way in which the test is set up.

This would be a better way of setting it up.

Tube 1   yeast + sugar + water in the warm
Tube 2   yeast + sugar + water in the fridge
Tube 3   yeast + water in the warm
Tube 4   yeast + water in the fridge

This would now be a fair test. If it was done more than once it would give more reliable results.

KEY WORDS

decay
yeast
fair test

 What results would you expect from the fair test described above?

TYPES OF MATERIAL

Different materials have different properties and are good for different jobs. Cars are made of steel because it is strong and easy to make into different shapes. Plastic is not strong enough to make a car, but it makes good furniture. We need to know how to pick the right material for each job.

- Different materials have different properties.
- There are reasons why particular materials are chosen for different jobs.
- We need to test materials to make sure they are suitable for a particular job.

See why each material was chosen for its job.

Electrical wire is usually made of the metal copper. This is because copper is a good conductor of electricity. It lets the electricity pass through easily.

The body of a plug or a light switch is usually made of plastic. Plastic is a good choice because it is an insulator. It will not let electricity pass through. That keeps you safe when you touch the plug.

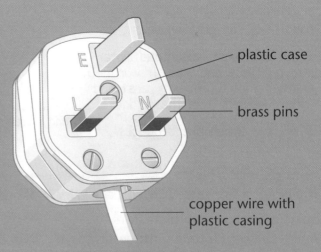

plastic case

brass pins

copper wire with plastic casing

Some materials are absorbent. They are able to soak up liquids easily. Some sorts of paper and cloth are absorbent, so they can be used to make towels to dry things.

Some materials are waterproof. Rubber and plastic are good for wellington boots because they keep water out!

 Choose a room at home. Look around and pick six different objects. Say what each one is made of, and what property of the material makes it a good choice.

Identifying which factors are important in a fair test

It's very important to test things in a fair way. It can be easy to make a mistake. You need to be clear about which factor you are testing. Change only this factor and keep everything else exactly the same.

Look carefully at Sara's experiment.

Sara had two rolls of kitchen paper towels – Super-sorb and Econo-wipe. She wanted to test them to see which was the more absorbent.

First I poured a tablespoon of orange juice onto the table. I put one square of Super-sorb on top and patted it down. Then I poured one tablespoon of tomato ketchup onto the table, put a square of Econo-wipe on top and patted it down.

When I picked up the square of Super-sorb, I saw it had absorbed all the juice, leaving a dry surface. When I picked up the Econo-wipe, it had absorbed some of the ketchup but there were still sticky bits left on the table.

Sara concluded that Super-sorb was the more absorbent material.

Was she right?

To have a fair test, you must decide which factor you are going to test, and then keep all the other factors the same. Sara was testing the absorbency of the different kinds of paper. She did use the same amount of paper and the same amount of substance, but she used two different substances – orange juice and tomato ketchup. It was not a fair test.

KEY WORDS

conductor
insulator
absorbent

What could you do to make this a fair test? Write down what you would do.

KEEPING WARM

Keeping ourselves warm is very important. We couldn't live for very long outside in the winter without our clothes and houses to keep us warm. Sometimes we want food and drinks to be kept hot. Other foods have to be kept cool and fresh – especially in the summer.

- Thermal insulators are materials that stop heat going through.
- The same materials will keep cool things cool and hot things hot.
- Objects always end up at the temperature of their surroundings.

Let's find out more about thermal insulators.

Air is a very good insulator. Materials that keep things warm often have lots of air spaces inside. Bubble wrap is good insulator, so is foam rubber.

Your clothes keep you warm because of the air trapped inside. An animal's fur traps air and keeps it warm. Feathers on a bird work in the same way.

Insulating materials stop heat from escaping, but they stop heat from getting in just as well. You can use a 'cool bag' to keep drinks cool or to bring frozen food home from the shops – but you could also use it to keep your fish and chips warm on the way home from the chip shop.

 Look around your house. Make a list of all the materials being used to keep something warm. Are any of materials on your list ever used to keep things cool?

Identifying anomalous results

By making a graph you can see your results more clearly. You can see, by looking at the graph, if there are any 'unexpected' results – ones that don't fit the pattern. Sometimes this might be because you have made a mistake taking a reading.

Take a look at these results.

Matthew did an experiment with a polystyrene cup. He wanted to see how good it was at keeping a drink hot. He compared it with a plastic cup of the same size. He started with each cup filled with water at 50 °C. Then he took the temperature of the water in both cups every minute.

Polystyrene cup	
Time minutes	Temperature °C
0	50
1	42
2	35
3	30
4	26
5	24
6	22
7	21
8	20

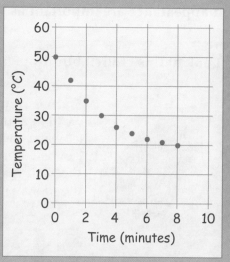

Graph to show liquid cooling in a polystyrene cup

Can you see that there is a problem with one of the results for the plastic cup? The two-minute reading looks much too high. Has the water really warmed up? It is more likely that something went wrong with the experiment. This is called an anomalous result. Matthew would have to repeat the experiment to check the measurements.

Plastic cup	
Time minutes	Temperature °C
0	50
1	40
2	42
3	26
4	22
5	21
6	20
7	20
8	20

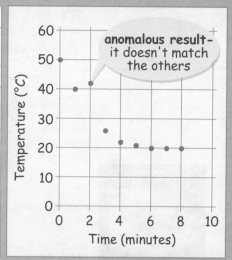

anomalous result – it doesn't match the others

Graph to show liquid cooling in a plastic cup

KEY WORDS

thermal insulator
anomalous result

Think about Matthew's experiment. What could have gone wrong? Write down your ideas.

ROCKS AND THEIR USES

There are many different kinds of rock. We use some of them for building. Some rocks are very hard, others are soft. Some are very easy to cut into shapes, others might be too hard or too crumbly to be of any use. Colour and appearance are important as well.

- Beneath the soil there are always rocks if we dig deep enough.
- Different rocks have different properties.
- Different rocks can be used for different jobs.

Look at this church building. See why each of the stones has been used.

Slate is very hard-wearing and will not let water through. It can be cut into thin sheets. It is ideal for the roof.

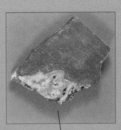

Marble is hard and shiny. It will last a long time and looks very attractive. It can be carved into many shapes.

Sandstone is a soft rock made of grains of sand which you can see if you look closely at the surface. It is attractive and easy to cut to shape.

Granite is very strong and hard. Stones cut from granite make very good building blocks.

Look at some of the some buildings near where you live. Find out which rocks have been used. Are they local, or have they been brought in from somewhere else?

Using a key correctly

You can use a key to identify rocks. You need to be able to answer some simple questions about the rock.

Look at this simple key that can be used to identify four rocks.

Can you scrape bits off easily with a metal spoon?

- **Yes**
  - Can you see shiny little grains?
    - **Yes** — It is sandstone
    - **No** — It is chalk
- **No**
  - Is it smooth and white?
    - **Yes** — It is marble
    - **No** — It is granite

Yasmin wanted to use the key to help her identify a piece of rock.

The first question was:

Can you scrape parts off easily with a metal spoon?

She tried and found that she couldn't scrape it, so the answer was 'no'. That took her to the next question:

Is it smooth and white?

As her rock was smooth and white, she answered 'yes'. That told her that the rock she had was marble.

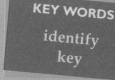

KEY WORDS

identify
key

Write down two characteristics you could use to identify sandstone. What is the name of a soft rock that does not have shiny grains in it?

SOLIDS, LIQUIDS AND GASES

Water can exist as a solid (ice), a liquid (water) and a gas (steam). Many other substances can also have these three states. We are used to seeing the metal iron as a solid, but it can also be a liquid (called molten iron) and even a gas if it gets hot enough.

- Solids keep the same shape and volume.
- Liquids take the shape of anything you pour them into.
- Gases will spread out to fill up any space they are in.

See how the way tiny particles behave makes the difference.

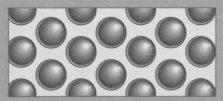

In a solid, the particles are fixed in their positions. That is why a solid keeps its fixed shape.

REMEMBER
A powder can be poured like a liquid but it is really a solid. It is made of tiny solid pieces.

The particles in a liquid can move around. That is why a liquid can take on any shape. It keeps the same volume.

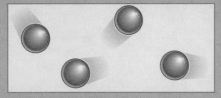

Gas particles are free to move around quickly. They spread out to fill the space available.

Sort this list into three groups: solids, liquids and gases: • iron • paper • syrup • sugar • air • steam • hair gel • orange juice • carbon dioxide • wood

Matching the right word to its description

It is important to use the correct scientific words for things. Each science word has a special meaning and needs to be used carefully.

Study these words and their descriptions.

solid • liquid • gas • powder • molten • particle

A	**B**	**C**
This is very soft and runs a little bit like a liquid, but it is dry to touch and the small pieces it is made of are solid.	If iron is made really hot it forms a liquid called _____ iron.	When something is in this state it does not have a fixed shape or size. It fills up any container.

D	**E**	**F**
This is one of the tiny pieces that all make up all matter.	This keeps its shape because its particles are fixed in place and cannot move around.	Cool this down and it freezes. Warm it up and it turns to a gas. It is runny and can be poured.

Jack wanted to match up the words and their definitions.
What clues could he find?

◆ Jack thought about pouring soap powder because it flows like a liquid, but each little bit is solid. So **A** is 'powder'.

◆ Jack knew that 'molten' is just another word for 'melted'. So in **B**, liquid iron must be 'molten'.

◆ Jack thought about pumping up a bike tyre to answer **C**. The air fills up the shape of the tyre. So **C** had to be 'gas', like air.

◆ Jack knew everything is made up of particles, so **D** is 'particle'.

◆ Jack thought about things that keep their shape like a brick or a piece of wood – they are solids so **E** is 'solid'.

◆ Jack thought about water freezing to ice, and boiling to steam. Water is liquid so **F** is 'liquid'.

KEY WORDS

solid
liquid
gas

**Look up the definition of each of these words in a dictionary.
Can you improve on the dictionary to make the definition more scientific?**

HEATING AND COOLING

Many substances can exist as a solid, a liquid or a gas. It is the temperature that makes the difference. If you heat up ice it will melt to liquid water, and then boil away to make steam. It works in reverse too. Cool the steam down and it will turn back to water, and then freeze to solid ice.

- Water freezes to ice at 0 °C, and boils into steam at 100 °C.
- Changing between solid, liquid and gas is called 'changing state'.
- When a liquid evaporates, the particles are escaping into the air as a gas.

REMEMBER
We often use the word freeze for when something gets very cold – but in science it is used for something changing state from liquid to solid.

These examples show changing state by heating and cooling.

On a cold window, water vapour condenses into water.

The heat from the flame melts the wax. Further down the candle it is cooler, so the wax freezes again.

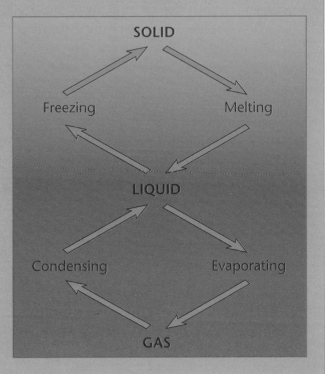

SOLID

Freezing   Melting

LIQUID

Condensing   Evaporating

GAS

Think about some washing drying out on the line. What change of state is happening? Where does the water go to after the clothes have dried?

Putting the right labels on a diagram

Diagrams are an excellent way of showing some types of information. They save a lot of words and are much clearer. They do need good labels – in the right places.

Let's look at the way changing state fits into the water cycle.

Mina had this good diagram of the water cycle. She wanted to make it clearer by putting in these words that describe change of state:

evaporation • condensation • freezing • melting

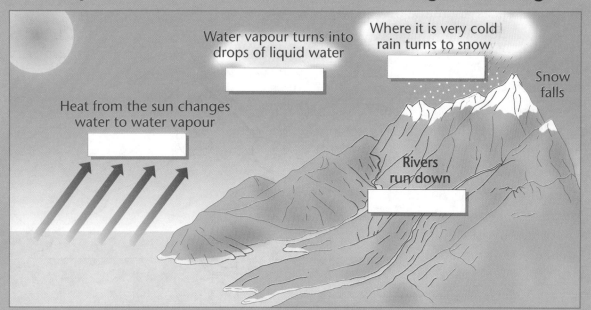

Water vapour turns into drops of liquid water

Where it is very cold rain turns to snow

Snow falls

Heat from the sun changes water to water vapour

Rivers run down

How could she decide where the labels should go?

◆ She realised that where water leaves the sea and moves up into the air as water vapour, it is evaporating. So 'evaporation' fits in here.

◆ High in the sky it is cold, so that is where water vapour turns back into water. She could write 'condensation' near the cloud.

◆ Rain turning to snow is 'freezing', so that will fit below the cloud.

◆ 'Melting' is where ice turns to water, so Mina put that below the snow line on the mountain.

KEY WORDS

condense
freeze
melt
boil

Find examples of those same four changes of state happening in your kitchen at home.

DISSOLVING

What actually happens to sugar when you dissolve it in a cup of tea? You can taste it in the tea, so it must still be there, but you can't see it any more. Where have the particles of sugar gone?

- When something dissolves it does not just 'disappear'. It is still in the liquid.
- The dissolved particles have found spaces in between the particles of water.
- Substances may dissolve quickly or slowly. Stirring speeds it up.

To understand how dissolving works, think about the particles that substances are made of.

The substance we are dissolving (such as the sugar) is called the solute.

The liquid we are dissolving it in (such as the water in the tea) is called the solvent.

Only three or four spoonfuls of sugar will dissolve. Any more just sinks to the bottom of the cup.

If a substance can be dissolved, then we say it is soluble.

sugar (solute)

water in tea (solvent)

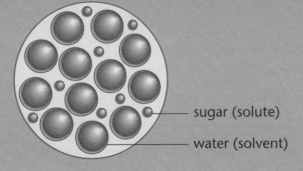

sugar (solute)

water (solvent)

The particles of solute are still there. They are in the spaces between the solvent particles.

You cannot see the dissolved substance any more but it is still there in the liquid.

Do all substances dissolve equally well? Test it out with salt and sugar. See how many spoons of sugar will dissolve in a glass of cold water. Make sure you measure out the same amount in each spoonful. Then try it again with salt. Which one is more soluble?

Designing a good experiment

How can you make your investigations really good? You need to plan and carry out your investigation carefully to get reliable results.

See how a basic idea for an investigation can be improved.

Daniel wanted to know if the temperature makes any difference to how much salt will dissolve in water.

The basic idea

I will measure the salt and stir it into cold water, counting how many spoons would dissolve before I have some left in the bottom. I will do it all again with warm water.

I will compare the two sets of results.

His write-up shows how he planned the investigation carefully.

A I think that warm water will dissolve more salt than cold water.

B I used the same beaker each time, and the same amount of water.

C I decided to do the whole thing twice in case I made a mistake.

D I found that warm water dissolves more salt than cold water

Here Daniel is making a prediction – writing down what he expects to happen.

This is to make sure he has a fair test.

Doing it all twice helps to make his results much more reliable.

This is Daniel's conclusion. He is stating what he has found out.

KEY WORDS

solute
solvent
soluble
prediction
conclusion

Think back to an investigation that you enjoyed doing in school. Write down your own versions of statements A to D for that investigation.

REVERSIBLE CHANGES

If water is frozen to make ice, it is easy to get the water back again. Just warm up the ice and it will melt to water. Freezing and melting are changes that can easily be reversed. A reversible change is not for ever; it is possible to get back to the thing you started with.

- A reversible change is where you can get back the thing you started with.
- Changes of state like melting and freezing are reversible changes.
- When a substance is dissolved, you can get it back by evaporating the water.

Look at these two changes that can easily be reversed.

A puddle is dried up by the Sun. Liquid water is evaporating to become water vapour.

A cloud forms in the cold air. Water vapour is turning into liquid water.

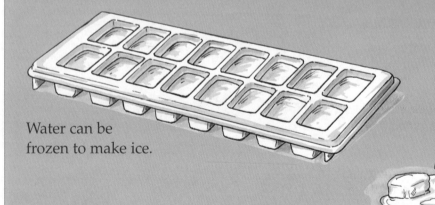

Water can be frozen to make ice.

In a warm room, ice turns back into water

Think about all the changes that happen in the kitchen. Write a list of reversible changes. Remember the rule: if you can somehow get back the thing you started with, then it is a reversible change.

Using scientific words when you can

It is possible to describe what you see in everyday words. You can describe them more accurately using the proper scientific words.

Look at how Sara improved her description by using the right words.

Sara had to describe what she knew about melting chocolate.

Here is her first attempt.

> I heated up some squares of chocolate in a saucepan. The chocolate went soft and then runny.
>
> When I left it to go cold again the chocolate went hard.
>
> Chocolate can go runny and back to hard.

Here is her second attempt.

> I heated up some squares of solid chocolate in a saucepan. The chocolate melted and became liquid.
>
> When I left the melted chocolate to cool down it became a solid again.
>
> Melting chocolate is a reversible change.

The second version is much better. Sara has added the correct scientific words – **solid**, **melted**, **liquid** and **reversible**. It has made her work much more accurate.

KEY WORDS

solid
melted
liquid
reversible

 Look at the writing in your science notebook. Are there any descriptions that you can improve, like Sara did, by using better words?

IRREVERSIBLE CHANGES

Sometimes when you heat something up, it changes in such a way that you cannot change it back again. If you cook an egg by boiling it in water, you can't turn it back into a raw egg by putting it into a refrigerator. Once the egg is cooked it will stay cooked forever. Many changes cannot be reversed.

- An irreversible change is where you cannot get back the thing you started with.
- When candle wax is burnt and becomes gas, it is an irreversible change.
- We can use irreversible changes to make useful new materials.

Now look at these irreversible changes.

When wood is burned it changes into new substances:

◆ a powdery solid called ash is left in the grate;

◆ small carbon particles float away as smoke;

◆ some invisible gases are also released into the air – the main ones are carbon dioxide and water vapour.

You could never get all of these new substances together and turn them back into wood.

If an acid such as vinegar is poured onto bicarbonate of soda, the crystals dissolve and a lot of bubbles are made. The bubbles are carbon dioxide.

You could not put the carbon dioxide back into the beaker and get the vinegar and bicarbonate of soda back again.

Sort these changes into two groups, reversible and irreversible:
- melting chocolate • making concrete • baking a cake • melting an ice cream
- burning gas in a gas fire • making ice cubes

Using scientific knowledge in a new situation

You learn about science in the classroom, but in fact science is going on all around you! Often, you don't have to look any further than your own home to find examples of the things you have learned about in science.

See how you can find reversible and irreversible changes in the kitchen.

While Tom was helping in the kitchen he noticed there were lots of changes taking place. He decided to make two lists – one for all the reversible changes and the other for all the irreversible ones.

Can you see how Tom made his decisions?

Each time he asked himself one simple question:

'Would it be easy to get back the thing or things I started with?'

For example, he knew that he could refreeze ice cream just by putting it back in the freezer.

On the other hand we can boil an egg by heating it, but if we cool it down again it is just a cold boiled egg! It can never become raw again.

Reversible changes
Defrosting ice cream
Heating up water
Dissolving sugar in tea
Melting chocolate

Irreversible changes
Boiling an egg
Cooking bacon
Baking a cake
Burning a match

KEY WORDS
reversible
irreversible

 See if you can find some more examples of reversible and irreversible changes in your kitchen for the lists.

SEPARATING BY SIEVING

Soil is made from crushed-up rock. Over many years the weather and running water break up rocks into tiny pieces. Other things mix in as well. There will be the remains of dead animals and plants, as well as some living things such as insects. How can we separate all these different parts?

- Soil contains particles of many different sizes, from fine dust to big stones.
- We can separate these particles by using sieves with different sizes of hole.
- Any mixture of different sized particles can be separated in the same way.

Soil can be separated with a sieve.

You can see the largest soil particles trapped in the top sieve. The pieces are so big that they can't even get through the large holes.

The next sieve has smaller holes so it traps smaller particles. These could be sand.

Only the tiniest pieces of clay can get through the really small holes in the final sieve.

Sieves could also be used to separate other mixtures. Here one is used to separate rice and sand.

 Are there any sieves in your kitchen at home? Find out what they are used for. Ask if someone will show you how they are used.

Using bar charts to make comparisons

Some results will be much easier to understand if you can set them out in a bar chart. You need to look carefully at the scale.

Look at the way Jamal used bar charts to compare two soil samples.

Jamal looked at some bar charts comparing two samples of soil. One sample came from a place where the soil was usually dry and easy to dig. The other type of soil was often wet and hard to dig.

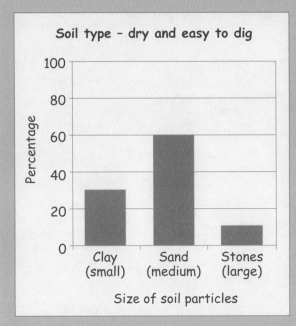

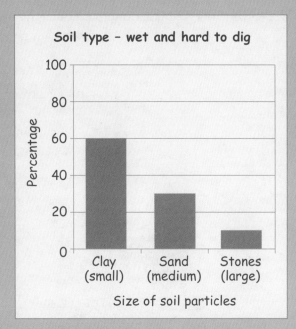

Bar charts showing soil composition

Can you see how the two charts showed Jamal the difference between the two types of soil in a very clear way? The taller bars mean a larger amount. On the bar charts, Jamal could easily see that:

◆ both types of soil had the same amount of stones – 10%;

◆ the soil that dried out easily had a large amount of sand in it – 60%;

◆ the soil that stayed wet and was hard to dig had a lot of clay – 60% – but much less sand – 30%.

Look through some newspapers. They often use bar charts to display their information. Cut some out and stick them in your science notebook.

SEPARATING BY FILTERING

Solids that do not dissolve in a liquid are called insoluble substances. Filtering is used to separate an insoluble solid, such as sand, from a liquid, such as water. It is used by scientists in their experiments. It can be used to clean up water – it can help make dirty water from a reservoir so it is fit for us to drink. How does it work?

- Filter paper has tiny holes that are too small to see but let water through.
- Pour dirty water through filter paper and dirt will be trapped in the paper.
- Huge filters made of sand and gravel clean up water in water works.

See you how you can use a paper filter to separate sand from water.

fold the paper once → fold it again → pull it out into a cone

To separate sand and water:

- Fold the paper into a cone shape.
- Put the paper cone into a funnel.
- Put the funnel over a container.
- Pour the mixture into the cone.

Using a filter

 Can you think of some other solids that can be separated from a liquid using a filter?

Interpreting a flow chart

Flow charts are very useful to explain something that works in stages, one step after the other. You can see the order of events very clearly.

Have a look at this flow chart. It shows the stages of cleaning water.

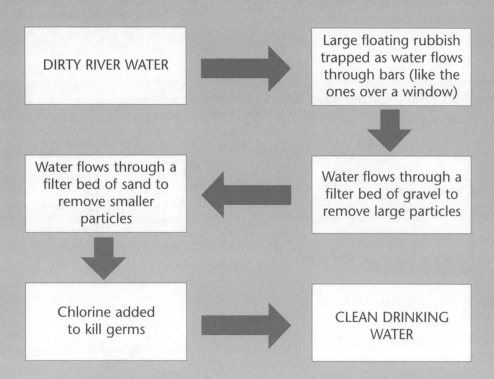

DIRTY RIVER WATER

Large floating rubbish trapped as water flows through bars (like the ones over a window)

Water flows through a filter bed of sand to remove smaller particles

Water flows through a filter bed of gravel to remove large particles

Chlorine added to kill germs

CLEAN DRINKING WATER

Using this flow chart, Topi can easily see how water is cleaned step by step, until it is ready to drink.

◆ She starts in the top left-hand corner with dirty river water.

◆ Then she just follows the arrows, reading each box as she goes.

◆ Starting with the largest objects, all of the dirt is removed by filters that have smaller and smaller holes.

◆ The last thing to happen is that chlorine is added to kill germs.

◆ Finally Topi sees that clean drinking water is shown in the bottom right-hand corner.

KEY WORDS

filter
filter bed
flow chart

Make a flow chart showing how to make a cup of tea. Start off with a box saying FILL THE KETTLE and finish with one saying DRINK TEA.

SEPARATING BY DISSOLVING

Some of the salt we use comes from salt mines under the ground. When it has been mined the salt is usually dirty – mixed up with sand and stones. The salt has to be cleaned up before it can be used in cooking. How can you use your knowledge of science to separate the salt from the sand?

- Salt is soluble because it dissolves in water, but sand is insoluble.
- Salt and sand can be separated by dissolving the salt in water.
- Mixtures can be separated by dissolving if one part is soluble and the other is not.

This method of separating uses filtering as well as dissolving.

1
Begin with a mixture of sand and salt. This is like the gritty salt we put on the roads in winter.

2
Add water and stir it well. The salt dissolves but the sand does not.

salty water

sand

3
Now the salt is dissolved in the water, and the sand is left at the bottom.

filter paper

sandy salt solution

sand trapped by filter

salty water

4
Finish off with a filter. The salty water runs through and the sand is held in the filter.

 Can you think of any other mixtures that could be separated by this method?

Matching the right word to its description

There are many new words to learn in science. It can seem like a lot to start with, but the best way is to learn a few at a time as you go along.

Learn the words in families. It helps you to remember them.

Clare sometimes sets new words out in a special way to remind herself of the words that go with a particular topic. It is called a mind map.

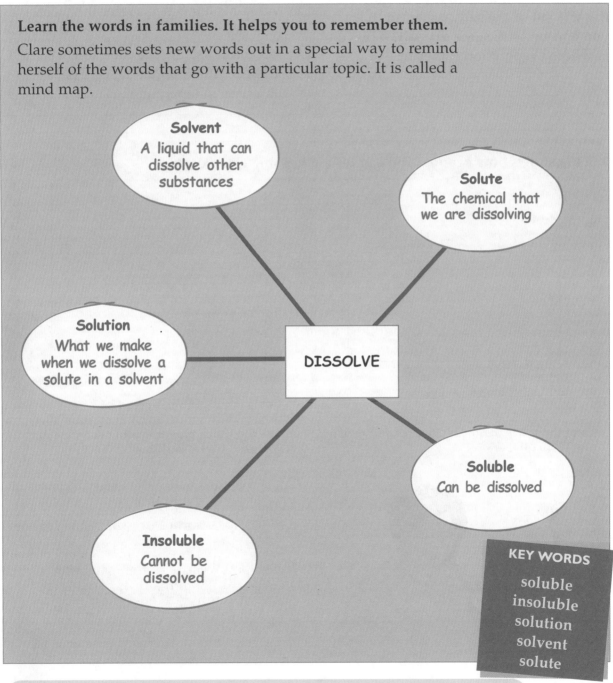

Solvent
A liquid that can dissolve other substances

Solute
The chemical that we are dissolving

Solution
What we make when we dissolve a solute in a solvent

DISSOLVE

Soluble
Can be dissolved

Insoluble
Cannot be dissolved

KEY WORDS

soluble
insoluble
solution
solvent
solute

Make yourself a mind map to show a set of words that go with another topic.
Put **FILTER** in your middle box and see how many words you can link to it.

SEPARATING BY EVAPORATING

On page 58, you saw how to use dissolving to separate some sand and salt. You would be left with clean salty water. But how could you get the salt out of the salty water, so that you end up with some dry salt? This is where evaporation comes in.

- You can get dissolved salt out of a solution by evaporating the water. You can do this by simply leaving the water. You can do it more quickly by boiling it.
- The salt is left behind after the water has evaporated.
- You could use evaporation to get sugar out of a cup of tea, or to see what is dissolved in lemonade.

This shows how evaporation can give you some clean dry salt.

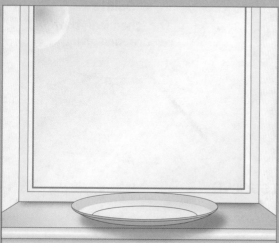

First the salt is dissolved. You cannot see it but it is still there.

When the water evaporates you see the salt left behind in the saucer.

All drinks are mainly water with various things dissolved in it. Read the labels of a few drinks bottles or cans. You will see a list of some of the things in the drink.

If you pour a little of the drink onto a saucer and let all the water evaporate, you will see what is in the drink besides water.

 Pour a little drink from a bottle or can into a saucer and leave it out for the water to evaporate. Describe what is left on the saucer.

Writing a good explanation

Once you have done your experiment you need to explain clearly what you have done. To do this well you need to use the right scientific language and be accurate.

Think about these explanations that Mr Smith collected in from his class.

The class had been studying evaporation. They had done the experiment on the opposite page, dissolving salt in water and then letting the water evaporate. They wanted to see if they could get the salt back.

Who has written the best explanation?

Matthew

...after a while the water just vanished.

This is not a clear explanation. Matthew doesn't say **exactly** how long it took. Also, *vanished* is not a scientific word – it sounds more like magic!

Topi

...by the afternoon the water had dried up.

This is better. Topi has given some idea of time, and *dried up* is accurate.

Clare

...after 4 hours the water had evaporated. We were left with dry salt.

This is the best. Clare has told us the **exact** time taken. She has used the correct word – *evaporate*. She has also told us what happened to the salt.

KEY WORDS

evaporation
explanation

Look back through your science notebook. Can you see any places where the words you used were not the scientific words? Can you think what would be the correct words to use?

DRAWING ELECTRICAL CIRCUITS

Electrical circuits contain components such as batteries, lamps and switches. When you look at diagrams of circuits, you will see that each component is always drawn with its own special symbol. Why is this important? Once you know the symbols, you can draw any electrical circuit you like. Other people will understand what you have drawn because everyone uses and understands the same symbols.

- Each component in an electrical circuit has its own symbol.
- Circuit diagrams are always drawn using these symbols.

Follow the path of the circuit in this torch with your finger.

Start at the battery and work your way around anticlockwise. The electricity moves from the battery straight into the lamp (bulb) and then along the wires and back to the battery. The switch completes or opens the circuit to switch the lamp on or off.

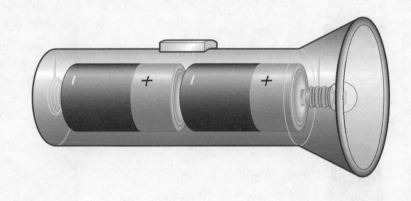

Here is the circuit diagram of the same torch. It is drawn using the correct symbols for the battery, switch, lamp and connecting wires.

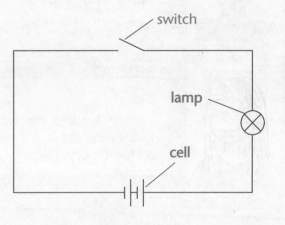

switch

lamp

cell

REMEMBER
Scientists always draw a circuit as a rectangle.

Find out the symbol for an electric motor. Draw an electrical circuit that contains a battery, a switch and a motor.

Following the convention

When people agree that they will all do something the same way, it is called a convention. The way electrical symbols are drawn is a convention. When you draw a circuit, it is very important to use the conventional symbols for electrical components. You can lose a lot of marks if you draw them wrongly.

Here are some of the correct symbols.

It is very easy to make mistakes like the ones shown here.
Make sure you don't do the same.

Cells

Batteries (more than one cell)

Lamps

Wires　　　　　　　　**Switches**

 Make a table with the correct symbols of some components in one column and the wrong symbols in another.

ADDING BATTERIES TO A CIRCUIT

A battery pushes electricity around the circuit. The electricity flowing around the circuit provides the power to make components such as light bulbs work. If the power the lamp needs is the same as the battery provides then it will light to its normal brightness. The components are then said to be matched. More power makes the lamp glow brighter and less power makes it glow dimmer. You can use these ideas to predict what might happen in a circuit you have not seen before.

- The brightness of a bulb or the speed of a motor in a circuit can be changed.
- This can be done by putting in a more powerful battery, adding extra batteries, or changing the number of lamps or motors in the circuit.
- The lamp or motor will burn out if there are more volts provided by the battery than are needed by the lamp or motor.

REMEMBER
A cell provides electrical power in a circuit. A battery is two or more cells together.

See how well these circuits work.

This circuit works very well. The electric motor was designed to work with a 3 volt battery. The two 1.5 volt cells add up to 3 volts, so the battery and the motor are matched. When the circuit is connected, the motor turns at its expected speed and does not overheat.

This circuit has the same motor as the first but the cell provides only 1.5 volts of energy. The circuit does work but the motor turns slowly. The components are not matched.

This circuit has the same motor as the first but it has a 4.5 volt battery which supplies too much power. The motor turns too quickly and gets very hot. Eventually it 'burns out' and stops working. The components are not matched.

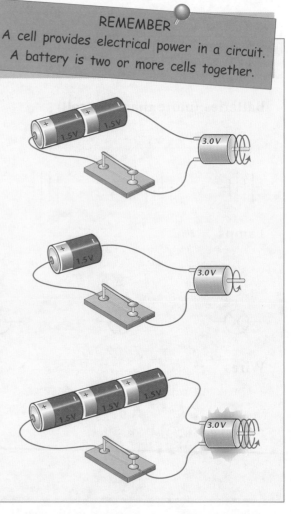

What is the difference between a matched and an unmatched circuit?

Making good predictions

When scientists plan an investigation, they usually think about what **might** happen. This is called a prediction. There are three stages in writing a good prediction:

- First think about what might happen when you do the test.
- Next think of a good reason why this might happen.
- Put it all together in an 'I think… because… ' sentence.

Help Clare finish her predictions.

Here are some circuits Clare has made. She has started to make some predictions about what might happen when she connects them.

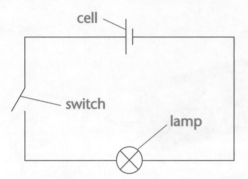

The lamp will light up because…

The lamp will become very bright because…

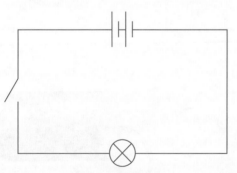

The lamp will get brighter because…

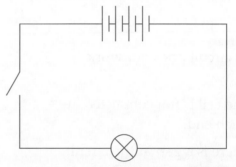

The lamp will burn out because…

KEY WORDS

circuit
matched component
prediction

Complete Clare's predictions using your knowledge of electrical circuits and correct scientific vocabulary.

WORKING ELECTRICAL CIRCUITS

Why do some electrical circuits work but others do not? For a circuit to work it has to have a cell or battery to supply the electricity. It has to have components such as bulbs, motors, and buzzers and these must be linked correctly by connecting wires. Circuits powered by cells are safe to use for carrying out fair tests.

- Working circuits contain components that are made of materials that are electrical conductors.
- A circuit must be complete, with no gaps, before it will work.
- A switch completes the circuit to turn it on and introduces a gap to turn it off.

Compare these two circuits.

This circuit works because:

◆ it has a good power supply;

◆ there is a complete circuit;

◆ the components are made of electrical conductors.

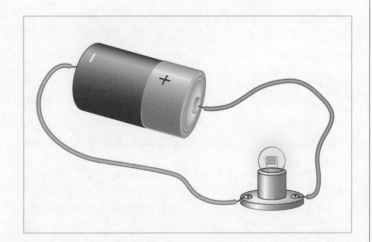

This circuit does not work because:

◆ the cell is not connected at each end;

◆ there is a gap in the circuit;

◆ one of the components is made of a material that is an electrical insulator (string).

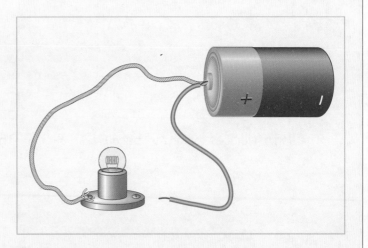

Use your knowledge of electricity to draw two circuits that will work and two that will not.

Making a test fair

Fair tests are very important. To make a test fair, you first need to identify all of the things that you **could** change in the investigation. These are called variables. Decide on just one variable – you will change this but keep all the rest exactly the same. Then your investigation will be a fair test of what happens when you change this one variable.

Now follow the way in which Tom set up his fair test.

Tom investigated an electrical circuit. He kept all of the components in the circuit the same except one. He changed the material he used to close the gap. Each time he changed the material, he looked to see whether the circuit worked or not.

This is what I kept the same	• the battery, the wires and the bulb
This is what I changed	• the kind of material in the gap
This is what I saw happen	• the bulb lit up when the paper clip, metal wire and drawing pin were put in the gap but not with the paper, matchstick or plastic pen

Can you see what Tom's results mean? The circuit worked only when it was complete and the gap was closed with a metal object. This made Tom think that all the metal objects were good electrical conductors because they made the bulb light up. The circuit would not work with the paper, wood and plastic – so these were not good electrical conductors. They are electrical insulators.

KEY WORDS

electrical conductor
electrical insulator

 Think of some other materials that would make the bulb light up if they were placed in the gap in the circuit.

MAGNETIC FORCES

A magnet is a metal that exerts a special force that can attract certain materials. There are only three metals that can be made into magnets – iron, cobalt and nickel. The ends of a magnet are called the poles and this is where the force is strongest. Some magnets are stronger than others and you can test for this.

Magnetic materials are different from magnets. Magnetic materials do not have magnetic force and so do not attract other materials but they are attracted by a magnet.

- Some materials are attracted to a magnet. These are called magnetic materials.
- Only the metals iron, cobalt and nickel can be made into a magnet.
- Two magnets can both attract (pull towards) and repel (push away from) each other.
- Some magnets are stronger than others.

Look at what these two magnets are doing to each other.

The ends of each magnet are called poles. This is where their magnetic force is concentrated.

One end is called the North pole and the other end the South pole.

When two North or two South poles face each other, the two magnets push each other away.

When a North and a South pole face each other, the two magnets attract each other.

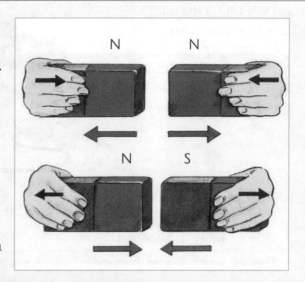

Remember the magnetic rule
LIKE POLES REPEL;
UNLIKE POLES ATTRACT.

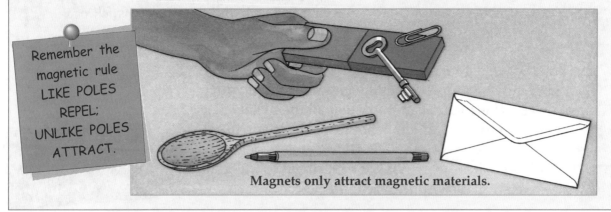

Magnets only attract magnetic materials.

What magnetic and non-magnetic objects can you find in your house? Make two lists and say what material each object is made from.

Making sense of data from a bar chart

Bar charts can sometimes be used to present the information you obtain from investigations. They contain a lot of information, set out clearly.

All bar charts present information in the same way:

- The title will tell you what is being investigated.
- The two axes will tell you what is being measured.
- The length of each bar will tell you the number of things which have been recorded.
- The labels will tell you the units the results are measured in.

Look at each part of this bar chart.

Jamal wondered how many paperclips could be picked up by magnets of different strengths. First of all he used one magnet. Then he made stronger magnets by joining together 2, 3 and then 4 magnets of the same strength. He made this bar chart to show the results.

KEY WORDS

magnetic
attract
repel

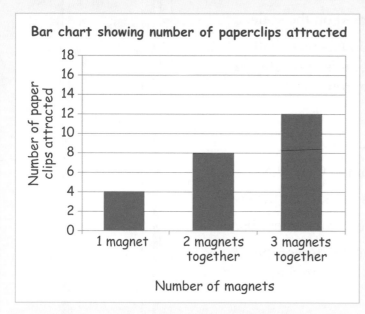

Can you spot:

◆ **the x-axis** (remember that is the one that goes across). This tells you the number of magnets he used.

◆ **the y-axis.** This shows the number of paperclips that the magnets picked up.

◆ **the first bar on the left**. This tells you that 1 magnet picked up 4 paperclips.

◆ **the second bar.** This tells you that 2 magnets picked up 8 paperclips.

◆ **the third bar.** This tells you that 3 magnets picked up 12 paperclips.

Now think carefully about the pattern Jamal found. Every extra magnet that is added picks up another 4 paperclips. So you would expect that 4 magnets would pick up 16 paperclips.

 Use the bar chart to work out how many paperclips would be attracted by five magnets joined together.

MEASURING WELL

In science, we use different equipment for measuring different things. To measure temperature, you would use a thermometer similar to the sort a nurse would use to measure your body temperature. Some equipment, such as a newton meter, is usually used only for measuring in science. A newton meter measures force.

- ○ Clocks measure time and volume can be measured using a measuring jug or cylinder.
- ○ Scales on scientific apparatus like thermometers and newton meters have to be read correctly.
- ○ Errors made when reading scales can lead to your investigation going wrong.

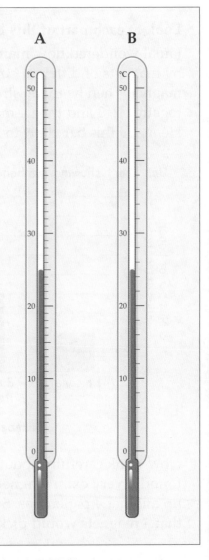

Learn how to read the scales on these thermometers.

Thermometers can be confusing to read.

Look first at thermometer A.

◆ It has a scale that goes from 0 °C to 50 °C.

◆ It is calibrated (marked) in one-degree intervals.

◆ It shows every 10 degrees marked on the scale.

◆ It reads 25 °C because the liquid has risen half way up the scale and the top of it is opposite the point which lies five marks up from the 20 °C mark.

Thermometer B is marked differently.

◆ It also has a scale that goes from 0 °C to 50 °C.

◆ It also shows every 10 degrees marked on the scale.

◆ It is calibrated (marked) in two-degree intervals.

◆ It also reads 25 °C but this time, the top of the liquid is two and a half marks up from the 20 °C mark.

REMEMBER
Always check the intervals on a thermometer so that you can read the scale correctly.

Draw a thermometer which has a scale going from 0 °C to 20 °C and is calibrated every 2 degrees Celsius. Show it measuring a temperature of 15 °C.

Avoiding mistakes when taking readings

It is easy to make mistakes when you take readings using scientific apparatus. You might read the scale wrongly or not precisely enough. Or you might read the measurement correctly but then write it down wrongly in your table of results.

Spot the errors in Sara's measurements.

Sara uses a newton meter to pull this box across different kinds of floor. Here is what each newton meter looked like when she took her measurements.

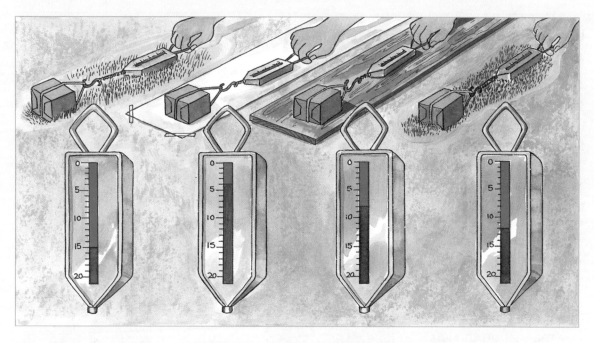

She is having a bad day. Look at the results she has written in her table.

Thick carpet	Plastic	Wood	Thin carpet
1.5 N	2 N	8 g	12 N

What did she do wrong? She read the scale wrongly in taking the first two readings. She wrote the third reading down wrongly and only got the fourth one correct.

KEY WORDS

calibrate
division
error
measurement

Read Sara's newton meters correctly and write the right results in your own table.

FORCES IN ACTION

What are forces? What can they do? Where do they come from? You cannot see forces but you can see what they can do. All objects have forces acting on them. Some forces are big and some are small. They are measured in newtons (N). You can record your measurements in tables which set out your data in an orderly way.

- Forces cause pushes, pulls, twists and turns.
- You can measure the size of forces using a newton meter.
- More than one force can act on an object. You can draw the forces acting on an object.

Look carefully at these force diagrams.

All objects have more than one force acting on them.

This bag of marbles is pulled down towards the centre of the Earth by the force of gravity. A second force from the hand pulls it upwards. The arrows show the direction of these forces.

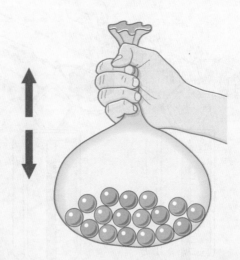

This paper clip has two forces acting on it. The magnet on the left pulls on it with an equal force to the magnet on the right. A force diagram also shows this.

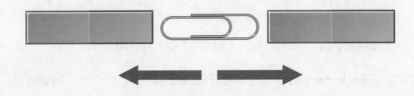

In both these diagrams the arrows are the same size which means the forces are the same size. They point in opposite directions and so the two forces act against each other.

REMEMBER
The length of each arrow shows the size of each force. The way the arrow points shows the direction it acts.

Draw two force diagrams – one to show the forces acting on a football on the ground and one for a paperclip hanging from a magnet.

Getting the right information from a table

The information in a table is set out in order and is easy to read. But you do need to know how to read it correctly.

Study the results in Daniel's table.

Objects always appear to weigh less in water than they do in air. Daniel wanted to investigate this. He measured the weight of some different materials in air and in water. Then he put his results in a table.

		Materials tested			
	Stone	Marble	Wood	Metal	Plastic toy
Weight in air (N)	4	2	7	10	3
Weight in water (N)	3	1.5	5	7	2.5
Difference in weight in water (N)	–1	–0.5	-2	3	-0.5

The two cells shaded yellow tell you that the stone weighs 4 N in air and 3 N in water.

Other cells in the first two rows tell you the weight of some other materials in air and in water.

Can you see the pattern? Each material weighs less in water than it does in air.

You can use the results to work out how much less the materials weigh in water.

The stone weighs 3 N in water and 4 N in air. So you can work out the difference in weight like this:
    4 N – 3 N = 1 N.

So Daniel wrote –1 N in the first cell in the bottom row. The minus sign simply means that it weighs less in water than in air.

Did he work his other results out correctly?

KEY WORDS

force diagram
gravity
newton

Draw the downward and upward forces acting on each of the objects in the table in air and in water. Remember to use arrows to show their size and direction.

STRETCHING SPRINGS

If you hold one end of a spring and pull the other end you will feel the forces acting on the spring. The spring will also stretch when you hold one end and add a weight to the other end. In each case you have two forces acting on the spring. Some springs are easier to stretch than others but the bigger the forces that act on a spring, the more it will stretch.

- Forces cause pushes, pulls, twists and turns.
- Weight is a force and it is measured in newtons (N).
- Sometimes results do not fit in with other results, and they need to be checked.

Think about the forces acting on these springs.

The spring stretches when you pull on each end of it.

The more you pull, the more the spring stretches.

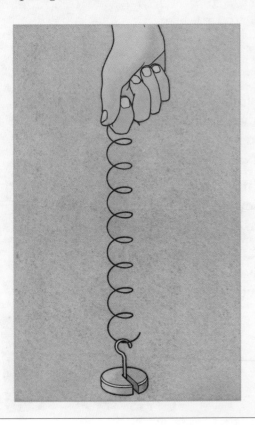

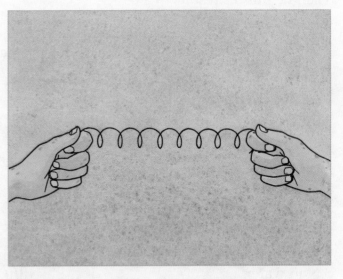

This spring has two forces acting on it – one from the right hand and one from the left hand.

The spring also stretches when you add weights to it. The weight is pulled towards the centre of the Earth by gravity and in turn pulls on the spring making it longer.

The more weights you add, the longer the spring becomes.

There is also another force on the spring. Your hand pulls the spring upwards in the opposite direction to the weight, pulling it down.

 Draw diagrams to show the forces acting on the two springs in the two pictures. Use arrows to show the direction and size of each force.

Spotting results which don't fit

Graphs help you to see if there is any pattern in your results. If your experimental data is good, then your graph will show a good pattern. However, you can make mistakes or even write your measurements down wrongly. These readings will not fit your pattern. It is usually easy to spot them.

Look carefully at Mina's graph.

Mina did an investigation in which she added different weights to a spring attached to a newton meter. Each time she added a weight, she recorded the reading on the newton meter and measured the length of the spring. She plotted the results on this graph.

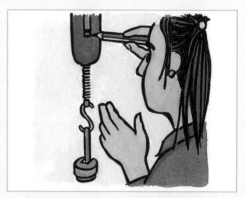

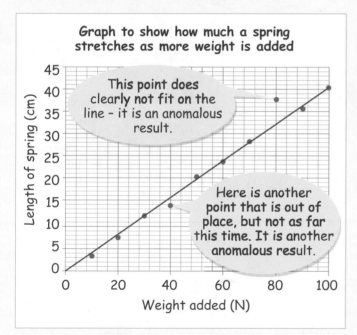

Graph to show how much a spring stretches as more weight is added

This point does clearly not fit on the line – it is an anomalous result.

Here is another point that is out of place, but not as far this time. It is another anomalous result.

Can you see how she has:

◆ used the x-axis for the scale for mass and the y-axis for the scale for weight;

◆ shown that the spring gets longer the more weight is added to it;

◆ shown that the spring gets longer by the same amount each time a weight of 10 N is added;

◆ drawn a line that goes through nearly all of the points.

Mina also noticed something odd. She was puzzled that two of the points did not fit on the line. Points like these, which don't fit the pattern, are called anomalous results. Usually they occur because something has gone wrong either with the investigation or with reading the results. In this case, Mina measured the length of the spring for the 40 N and 80 N weights wrongly.

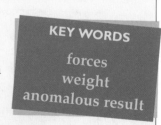

KEY WORDS

forces
weight
anomalous result

Draw Mina's graph again, putting in your estimate of the length of the spring for the 40 N and 80 N weights.

FALLING THROUGH AIR

Why do some objects fall more slowly through the air than others? Two forces act on every falling object. Air resistance pushes up on the object but gravity pulls it down. If there were no air resistance, the object would fall quite quickly. When there is air resistance, it takes longer to fall. The size of the air resistance and the time it takes to fall are related.

- Friction is a pushing force. It pushes against moving objects.
- Air resistance is a friction force that slows down objects as they move through air.
- The bigger the air resistance, the slower an object falls.

Spot the two forces on these objects as they fall.

The force of gravity on the two pieces of paper is the same.

The flat sheet of paper has a larger surface area than a screwed-up one. It has greater air resistance which slows the sheet of paper down as it falls.

The screwed-up piece of paper has less air resistance which slows the fall down, but not nearly as much as with the sheet of paper.

A real parachute falls slowly through air. This is because the canopy has an extremely large surface area which has a very large air resistance. This greatly slows the rate at which it falls.

REMEMBER
Air resistance is the force slowing the parachute down. Don't use the word upthrust, it's not the same thing.

 Draw a picture to explain what would happen to a coin and a feather when they fall on the Moon where there is no air resistance.

Writing a good relationship

When you do a fair test as part of an investigation, you usually end up with a conclusion which might be written something like this:

> The bigger the air resistance, the longer it takes an object to fall.

This is called a relationship. To write a good relationship you need to say how one variable affects the other, using words like bigger and smaller.

Follow how Matthew learnt to write a good relationship.

Matthew did an investigation to find out the effect of weight on the time it took a spinner to fall. He made sure the test was fair. He kept the kind of spinner, and the height he dropped it from, the same. He only changed the number of paperclips on the spinner to increase its weight. Finally, he measured the time it took each spinner to fall and wrote the results in a table.

Number of paper clips on the spinner	1	2	3	4	5
Time taken to fall (s)	3	2.8	2.7	2.6	2.5

Then he wrote his first attempt at the relationship.

> The spinner falls the quickest when five paperclips are put on it.

This is a true statement – but it doesn't explain the relationship. It only talks about one of the results, the last one in the table. Matthew looked again at the pattern in his results, and asked, 'When I change the number of paperclips, how does the time it takes the spinner to fall change?'

Then he tried to write the relationship again.

> The lower the number of paperclips on the spinner, the longer it took to fall.

This is really good because it describes the pattern and tells you exactly how changing one factor (variable) affects the other. Can you see where he used 'er' words to help?

KEY WORDS

air resistance
gravity
factors
relationship

Write a relationship that sums up how long parachutes of different sizes take to fall through air.

SHADOWS AND REFLECTIONS

Some people think that shadows and reflections are the same thing. Don't make the same mistake – they are very different from each other. You can only see the dark shape of an object in a shadow. In a reflection you can see a clear image of the object just as it appears in real life. Can you explain how each are formed using the idea of light rays?

- Light travels in straight lines. It cannot bend or travel around objects.
- When light is blocked, shadows are formed. When light hits a shiny surface, a reflection is formed.
- You can explain reflections and shadows by drawing the path that light rays travel.

Look at the ways in which a shadow and a reflection are different.

Shadows:

◆ form when light is blocked by an object;

◆ are created behind the object;

◆ are not the same colour as the object;

◆ show no pattern or detail – just the overall shape;

◆ do not swap left for right in the image.

Look at how the object blocks the light and forms a shadow.

Reflections:

◆ form when light from an object is reflected from a shiny surface;

◆ are created in front of the object;

◆ are 'lifelike' : they show the same colour and detail as the object;

◆ swap left for right in the image.

REMEMBER
Always draw light rays with an arrow in the centre pointing in the direction the light is travelling.

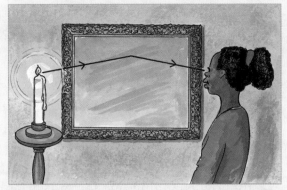

Look at how the light rays are reflected in the mirror so that Topi can see the image.

 Make a table that shows three ways in which shadows and reflections are different.

Explaining well

Explaining things well in science helps other people to understand why something happens. Good scientific explanations always contain good reasons and the correct scientific words.

To write a good explanation:

- make sure you give good reasons;
- use the correct scientific words and ideas;
- write concisely – don't waste words.

Use phrases such as these:

- This happens because…
- The reason for this is that…
- Since… then…

Follow the way Topi improved her explanation.

Topi tried to explain why cardboard makes a dark shadow and a plastic sheet makes a faint shadow. She started by writing:

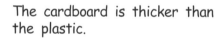
The cardboard is thicker than the plastic.

This only describes a property of cardboard and plastic. It contains no scientific ideas and does not give any explanation. She made another attempt.

The plastic lets more light through.

This is a better description and it gives a reason. However, it does not explain things well and does not use scientific words.

The reason why the shadows are different is that the plastic is translucent and so allows more light through than cardboard which is an opaque material.

This is the best! Now she had clearly explained why the shadows are different, giving good reasons and using the right scientific vocabulary.

KEY WORDS

opaque
shadow
reflection
translucent

Explain why shadows are formed behind objects. Use the idea of light rays.

CHANGING THE SIZE OF SHADOWS

What makes shadows change size? You can carry out fair tests to discover what factors make shadows bigger or smaller. As in all fair tests you need to make sure that you identify all the factors that could change. Then change just one factor whilst keeping the others the same. The more reliable your results, the better your conclusion will be.

- When light is blocked by an object, a shadow is formed.
- Shadows are always formed behind an object on the opposite side from which the light shines.
- Shadows will be bigger if you make the distance between the object and the light source smaller.

This is an investigation to find out how the size of a shadow changes as the distance between the torch and the model changes. The results have been put in the table for you to see.

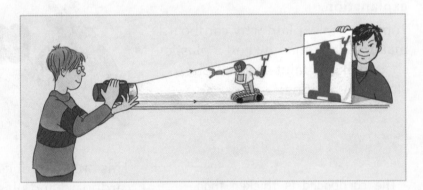

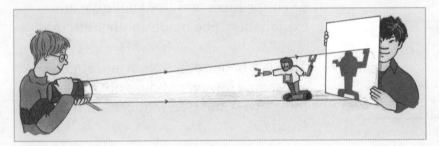

The test is fair because the distance between the object and the screen is always the same. The torch is always shone at the same angle.

Distance between the torch and the model (cm)	20	40	60	80	100
Size of the shadow (cm)	95	50	31	24	20

Look at the sizes of the shadows in this table. Can you spot any pattern? Look carefully! You will see that the nearer the model is to the torch, the bigger the shadow.

Check whether there is a regular pattern in the results by putting them into a line graph on your computer. Do all the points fit well?

Making your results more reliable

Once you have made your test fair, by controlling all the variables, you cannot make it any fairer. Some people think you can make it fairer by taking more readings. This is not true! Taking more readings does, however, make the results more reliable.

Look at how Jack got some more reliable results.

Jack wanted to see how the size of shadows changed when he changed the distance between his model and the screen where the shadow formed. Everything was as fair as it could be.

Here are his first results.

Distance between the model and the screen (m)	1.0	1.25	1.5	1.75	2.0
Size of the shadow (cm)	10	12	15	18.5	21

From these results he could see that the shadow got bigger as he moved the screen away from the object. But he was worried that his results did not fit into a good pattern. So, he repeated his investigation. This time he took four readings for each distance and worked out an average of the results.

Distance between the model and the screen (m)	1.0	1.25	1.5	1.75	2.0
Size of the shadow (cm)	10.1 : 9.8 9.9 : 10.2	12.1 : 12.9 12.2 : 12.8	14.9 : 15.1 15.5 : 14.5	18.5 : 16.9 17.1 : 17.5	21 : 19 19.2 : 20.8
Average size of shadow (cm)	10	12.5	15	17.5	20

Can you see how taking more readings and then taking an average improves the results and shows a better pattern?

 Draw line graphs of Jack's results in his two tests to show how his second results are better.

SOUNDS AND VIBRATIONS

You can hear many different kinds of sound. Animals make sounds, so do your stereo and all kinds of musical instruments. Sounds are produced in different ways. Have you ever wondered how sounds are made and how you come to hear them? What do they have in common? How are they different?

- Sounds are made when solids, liquids or gases vibrate.
- You can change the vibration and change the sound that is made.

Think carefully about what is vibrating here.

The tight skin on a drum vibrates very quickly. If you put some rice on the skin you can see the vibrations making the rice jump up and down.

When you tap a tuning fork on a hard surface it vibrates.

You can see it vibrating if you put it in water. The vibrations make the water splash all over the place.

REMEMBER
Sounds are made when a material vibrates.

Think of all the sounds you can hear at home. Make a table which shows where each sound comes from and what is vibrating to make the sound.

Seeing if the evidence fits your predictions

Making predictions helps you to think about what might happen in a scientific investigation. If your results support the prediction, then you have found an idea or general rule that fits the facts. Sometimes your prediction will not be backed up with the evidence that you find.

Look at how Yasmin compared her results with her predictions.

Yasmin noticed how the pitch of the note changed when she blew over some bottles with different amounts of water in them. She predicted that 'the pitch of the notes would get higher when there was more water in the bottle'.

She thought that this would happen when she tapped the bottles and when she blew over the top of the bottles. Then she tapped and blew over each one and recorded how the pitch changed.

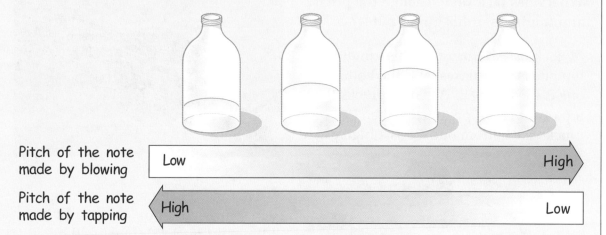

Pitch of the note made by blowing — Low → High

Pitch of the note made by tapping — High ← Low

Can you see why Yasmin was happy about how the pitch of the note changed when she blew across the top of each bottle? Blowing makes the air inside each bottle vibrate. Adding more water makes the column of air shorter. So, the shorter the column of air, the higher the pitch of the note. This fitted her prediction very well.

But Yasmin was very surprised that tapping the bottles gave the opposite pattern. Her teacher asked her what else could vibrate. She realised that when the bottle was tapped it was the water that vibrated. The longer the column of vibrating water, the lower the pitch of the note. Her prediction was wrong but she could explain the science.

KEY WORDS

vibration

Make a list of five musical instruments. What causes the vibration in each one? How do you change their pitch?

HIGH AND LOUD SOUNDS

What is the difference between a high and a loud sound, or between a low and a quiet sound? Many people get these confused. When you say a sound is high or low, you are talking about the pitch. When you say a sound is loud or quiet you are talking about the volume. Scientific ideas can be used to explain the things you experience in everyday life.

- Sounds have a high or a low pitch. They also have a loud or quiet volume.
- You can change the pitch and loudness of sounds.
- Making a vibrating string shorter, thinner or tighter makes the pitch higher as the vibrations are more frequent. Plucking it harder makes it louder because it makes the vibrations bigger.

What does Jack do to change the pitch and loudness of his guitar notes?

▼ Jack has six strings on his guitar. The top one is the thickest and the bottom one is the thinnest. When he plucks the top one it has a low pitch. When he plucks the bottom one it has a high pitch.

▲ He tunes his guitar by making each string tighter or looser until it is at the right pitch. Tightening the string raises the pitch and loosening the string lowers the pitch.

▼ He plays a tune by putting his fingers on the frets. As he moves his fingers up the frets, the pitch of the note is raised.

He can make the note louder by plucking the string harder and softer by plucking it move gently.

Make a list of everyday sounds. Which ones are loud or quiet? Which have a high or a low pitch?

Using your ideas in new situations

Sometimes when you do a test paper, you'll come across a question which is unfamiliar. Don't panic! Think about the things you have already learnt about the topic. Apply those ideas to the new problem.

See how Jack solved a problem using what he already knew.

Jack could play a guitar but not a recorder. He wondered how you change the pitch of the notes on a recorder. Look at how he worked on the problem. First he tried playing different notes. The black dots show you where he placed his fingers on the recorder.

Then he thought that it might help to work out what is vibrating when you blow into the recorder.

> I know my guitar makes a sound because the strings vibrate when I pluck them. So what vibrates in a recorder? It has no strings. So it must be air because blowing through the mouthpiece makes the air vibrate inside the tube.

> So how does the pitch of the notes change? On my guitar, the shorter the vibrating string, the higher the pitch of the notes.

Does something similar happen in a recorder? My theory is that the shorter the column of vibrating air inside the recorder, the higher the pitch will be. Now I can use this idea to work out the pitch of the recorder notes.

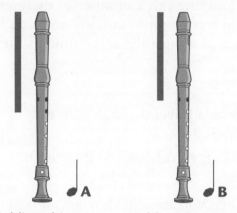

Holding this note gives a short column of air in the recorder.

Holding this note gives the shortest column of air in the recorder.

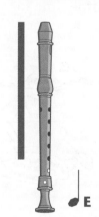

Holding this note gives a long column of air in the recorder.

Holding this note gives the longest column of air in the recorder.

KEY WORDS

pitch
vibration

Put the notes in order of pitch, starting with the lowest and ending in the highest.

TRAVELLING SOUND

Many materials vibrate and make a sound. If you are to hear the sound, it has to travel from where it is made, through anything which is in the way and into your ear. Sometimes sounds travel a long way and through a number of different materials. Sound travels quite quickly and you hear most sounds at almost the same time as they are made.

- Sounds can travel through solids, liquids and gases.
- Some materials let sounds pass through them better than others.
- You can draw a flow chart to show how sounds travel from one place to another.

Sounds travel through different materials.

Sounds travel quite well through gases.

When you are outside you can hear sounds from your friends, the birds and many other things around you. The sound travels through the air. Distant sounds take a little time to reach you.

Sounds travel even better and move quickly through liquids.

Dolphins and whales communicate with each other by sending high-pitched sounds through water. Sounds can travel a long way through water.

Sounds travel best through hard, solid material.

If you put your ear near to a radiator that is not too hot, you can hear the water circulating inside. The sound goes to your ear by travelling through the metal in the radiator.

Make a list of ten sounds you have heard today. Decide if they are made by a solid, liquid or gas vibrating. Put your ideas together in a table.

Making and completing a flow chart

Flow charts contain a sequence of information put together in the correct order. It helps you to follow the ideas.

Follow the steps in making your own flow chart.

Look at this diagram very carefully. Jack is playing his guitar and thinking about how the sound gets from the guitar to his ear. He thinks about all the different things that vibrate as the sound travels to his ear.

air vibrates

ear drum vibrates

guitar string vibrates

body of the guitar vibrates

Now you can start thinking about making the flow chart.

◆ First, identify all of the things that vibrate from guitar string to ear.

◆ Then, draw enough boxes to hold all the items of information.

◆ Next, write the information about the different vibrating materials in the correct order in the boxes.

◆ Finally, show where each vibration starts and finishes by arrows between the boxes.

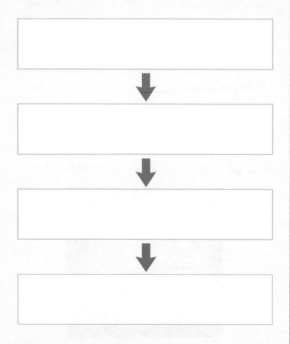

KEY WORDS

vibration

Make a new copy of Jack's blank flow chart and complete it. Then make your own flow chart to show how one of the sounds you are hearing now gets to your ear.

SUN, MOON AND EARTH

The Sun is a star at the centre of our solar system. The Earth is one of nine planets that orbit around it. The Moon is the only satellite to orbit the Earth. Over the past 500 years scientists have gathered more evidence about the Sun and the planets. We now know how big they are, how they travel and spin, their true shape and how far away they are.

- The Sun, the Moon and the Earth are roughly spherical.
- Photographs and other evidence can reveal the true shape of the Earth, Moon and Sun.
- The Moon travels around the Earth every 28 days.
- You can use a sequence of ideas to explain why you always see the same side of the Moon.

Look at the evidence for the Earth being spherical.

Many years ago most people thought the Earth was flat. But the evidence shows that this is wrong. The Earth is almost a sphere, just like a ball.

You cannot explain why ships sail over the horizon and around the world using the idea that the Earth is flat, but you can if you say that it is spherical.

Yuri Gagarin, the Russian cosmonaut, was the first man to travel in space. As he travelled around the Earth he could see that it was a sphere. People had worked out that the Earth was a sphere a long time before this, but he was the first person to see this for himself.

The best evidence that the Earth is spherical comes from photographs. Now everyone is able to see for themselves the true shape of the Earth.

Through photographs, we have discovered that the Earth is actually slightly pear shaped, with the North half being a little more pointed than the South half.

 Go on the Internet to the site http://antwrp.gsfc.nasa.gov/apod. This shows the astronomy picture of the day. Look at some more views of the Sun, Earth and Moon.

Explaining a sequence of ideas

Sometimes you can use one simple idea to explain your observations. More often, you have to give an explanation using a number of ideas put together in a logical way.

Gather the facts and link the ideas.

Have you ever wondered why you always see the same side of the Moon from Earth? Most people cannot explain this. You can if you get your facts right and use them well. Mina wanted to write an explanation. These were the facts she found.

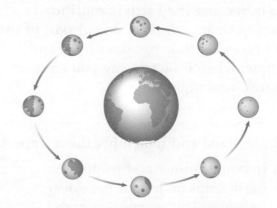

◆ You only see the Moon when the part of Earth you are on faces away from the Sun and it is night-time.

◆ You always see the part of the Moon which is lit up by the Sun.

◆ The Moon also makes one complete turn on its axis once every 28 days.

◆ The Moon orbits the Earth and makes one complete orbit every 28 days.

Then she used the ideas to link her explanation together.

First she stated the main reason.

> The reason why you see the same side of the Moon is that the Moon turns once on its axis in exactly the same time as it takes to circle the Earth.

Then she linked the ideas together to show how it works.

> Imagine it is the first day of the month and you can see a full Moon in the sky. The next night the Moon has moved a little around its orbit around the Earth. But it also turns a little on its axis, keeping the same part of the Moon facing you. This happens day after day. So, fourteen days later when the Moon has gone half way around its orbit of the Earth, it has itself turned half way around on its axis. After 28 days everything is back at the start position.

KEY WORDS

axis
orbit
spherical

Ask two or three people if they can explain why we always see the same side of the Moon. If they don't, teach them what the explanation is.

SUNRISE AND SUNSET TIMES

The Sun appears to rise in the morning, move across the sky during the day and then sink below the horizon in the evening. But it is really the Earth that moves and not the Sun. This is because the Earth is continually spinning on its axis. When your part of the Earth faces the Sun you have light and daytime; when it faces away you have darkness and night-time.

- The times of sunrise and sunset change during the course of the year.
- In winter the Sun rises late and sets early. In summer the Sun rises early and sets late.
- You can draw graphs to show how sunrise and sunset times change during the year.

Understand and remember these important facts.

◆ In both summer and winter, the Earth spins on its axis once every 24 hours. This means that each half of the Earth spends part of the time in sunlight and part in darkness

◆ There is more daylight in summer because the Sun is high in the sky. It is above the horizon for the greater part of the day.

◆ There is less daylight in winter because the Sun is much lower in the sky. It stays below the horizon for the greater part of the day.

REMEMBER
The Sun always rises in the east and sets in the west.

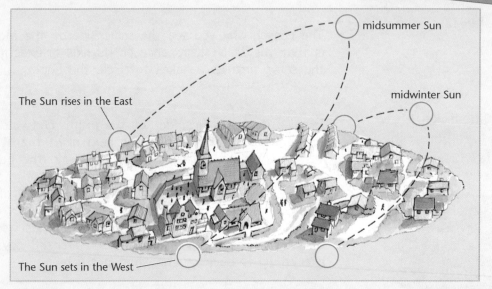

midsummer Sun

midwinter Sun

The Sun rises in the East

The Sun sets in the West

Go to the web site http://www.sunrisesunset.com/ Print off the sunrise and sunset times for London. Can you spot any pattern in the times you find?

Getting information from a graph

A graph is often a very good way of showing the pattern in your experimental data. Drawing a good graph requires skill – you need to know the right way to present all the information.

- The x-axis and y-axis will tell you what is being measured.

- On each axis there are scales with divisions that help you read the information.

- Each point is drawn using two pieces of data.

- The shape and pattern of the points help you talk about the relationship in the data.

Look carefully Sara's graph.

The graph Sara has drawn shows how the times of sunrise and sunset change during the year. All of the times are in the 24 hour clock format. So 08:00 is 8 o'clock in the morning, 12:00 is 12 o'clock midday and 20:00 is 10 o'clock at night. All times are in Greenwich Mean Time (GMT).

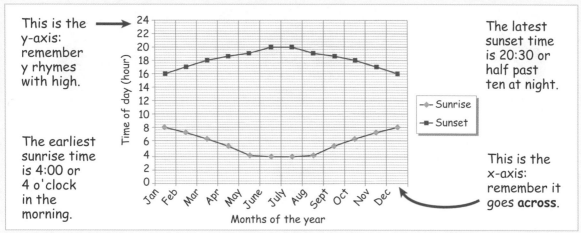

This is the y-axis: remember y rhymes with high.

The earliest sunrise time is 4:00 or 4 o'clock in the morning.

The latest sunset time is 20:30 or half past ten at night.

This is the x-axis: remember it goes **across**.

Graph of sunrise and sunset times during the year

Can you see how sunrise gets earlier between January and July and then gets later between July and December? Sunset time gets later from January to July and then gets earlier from July to December.

Sara also used the graph to find out how much daylight there is in the longest day. The longest day happens in July when the sun rises at around 4 o'clock in the morning and sets at 10 o'clock at night. So altogether there are 18 hours of daylight.

KEY WORDS

Earth's axis
sunrise
sunset

How many hours of daylight are there in the shortest day? Use the graph to read the sunrise and sunset times for the first day of each month.

THE MOVING EARTH

The Earth moves in two ways. First, it circles (or orbits) the Sun once every year. It does not move in an exact circle around the Sun. Its orbit is more like an ellipse. Although you don't feel as if you are moving at all, you are travelling through space at a very great speed! The Earth also spins on its axis, once every 24 hours. This is how we get night and day.

- The Earth moves around the Sun once every year, spinning as it goes.
- The Earth takes 24 hours to spin once on its axis.
- You must use the correct words when talking about the orbit of the Earth.

Look at how the Earth moves around the Sun.

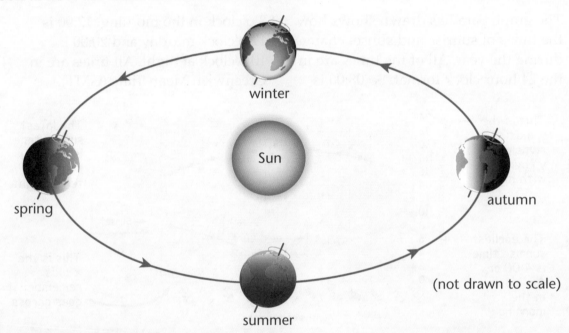

(not drawn to scale)

- If you could look from a point above the solar system, you would see the Sun with the Earth travelling around it.

- The Earth's axis is an imaginary line that runs from the North to the South pole.

- The Earth moves around the Sun in an anticlockwise direction.

- The Earth spins on its axis once every 24 hours.

REMEMBER
A year is 365¼ days and runs from one of your birthdays to the next.
Every four years an extra day is added to the calendar and we have a 'leap' year of 366 days.

 Explain why we add an extra day to the month of February every four years.

Using the right word

It is always better to use a science word rather than an everyday word when you label a science diagram. But it is important to make sure you are using the right idea before you put the label on. If you have got the wrong idea then you will probably write the wrong label.

Look how Jamal thought about the words to label the diagram.

Jamal has been given a diagram of a spinning Earth to label. It shows one half of the Earth in sunlight and the other half in darkness. The Earth is turning anticlockwise.

He has these words to choose from:

sunrise • line • midnight • equator • axis • 12 o'clock • morning • sunset • midday

D–E
This line is the Earth's axis. I didn't make the mistake of confusing it with the equator.

A
This point could be labelled 12 o'clock or midnight. I chose midnight because 12 o'clock could also mean midday.

C
This point could be labelled 12 o'clock or midday. I chose midday because it is more scientific.

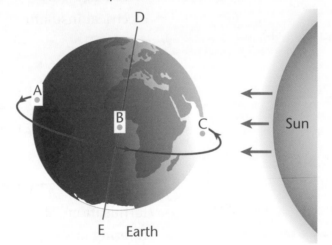

Sun

Earth

B
At this point the Earth is moving into daylight. The clue is the arrow showing the Earth moving anticlockwise. So I labelled this one sunrise and not sunset or morning.

Learn from Jamal. Always try to use the best scientific word. Look for clues in the diagram and watch out for words that can easily get mixed up. Label the words you know first, then do the other ones.

KEY WORDS

axis
orbit

Make your own drawing of the spinning Earth, showing daytime and night-time. Put as many labels on it as you can.

INDEX